Strategies of American Water Management

Gilbert F. White

Strategies of American Water Management

Ann Arbor
The University of Michigan Press

TO ANNE

Preface

In a country where parching drought, stinking streams, and muddy floods stimulate both scare headlines and the budgetary energies of legislatures there is no need to justify the critical study of water management for human good. An explanation is in order for appraising American experience in water use and control from an unconventional viewpoint at this time.

Notwithstanding public cries of impending water shortage, there is little reason to fear serious economic dislocations through failures in water quantity. The likelihood that the quality of human life will be impaired by misuse and degradation of the quality of available water is much greater. There is no realistic prospect that the community pulse of Los Angeles will ebb slowly to a halt or that New Yorkers will fall gasping of thirst on their grimy pavements through lack of water in the United States. Quantity seems manageable in the foreseeable future, although not without difficulties. Quality is less predictable. But deteriorated quality need not be decisive in influencing the course of regional development or national well-being. As the more promising storage sites are built up with concrete and earth structures on our streams, large and small; as the size of suggested remedial works reaches the colossal proportions of a Rampart Dam or a Columbia River-to-Kansas trans-basin diversion scheme; and as the results of multipurpose basin developments spread out in a great visible array from the upper Connecticut to San Diego, it is becoming apparent that a change in orientation of public efforts in water management is needed and is, in fact, taking shape. There is growing doubt that public aims of national efficiency, regional growth, and landscape preservation are being as well served as they might be.

The creation of the national Water Resources Council under the Water Resources Planning Act of 1965 was hailed as a major step forward in the rational, balanced use of the water resource. It provided for the first time since the demise of the National Resources Planning

Board in 1943 a formal executive agency through which diverse interests of the state and federal governments in water planning and operations could be coordinated. Ironically, no sooner was the Council organized and in operation than public recognition grew of the need for a different kind of mechanism which could become the vehicle for critical reassessment of the policies which the Council was coordinating and of the methods which it was helping the federal and state agencies to apply more efficiently in a basin-wide context. Congressional and executive discussion of a national water commission brought to light the desirability of a national group which would seek to appraise current management efforts against present and prospective conditions and to suggest major shifts in emphasis both as to techniques and as to regions of operation. In this situation, it may be helpful to ask what strategies for managing water seem to have emerged to date and what effects they have had on American society and on the landscape of a continent.

One conventional and perhaps fundamental way to analyze water management is to appraise from an administrative standpoint the long-run effort to achieve multiple purpose drainage basin planning for social aims. The concept of integrated river development has achieved recognition as an attractive goal since the Inland Waterways Commission Report of 1908, and it has dominated the public statements, if not the daily action, of water planning agencies over the past three decades. To ask how well the United States has moved toward this integrated type of planning might isolate the major issues, but there are several considerations that discourage it. That approach has been pursued thoughtfully by scholars as well as by government commissions. Sophisticated economic analysis also has been exercised fruitfully in sharpening thought about the contributions of water development to national economic efficiency. Research needs have been canvassed by committees of the Federal Council on Science and Technology, the National Academy of Science—National Research Council, and the American Geophysical Union. The comprehensive effort of the Senate Select Committee on National Water Resources in 1961 still is authoritative in its treatment of the nation's water supply and prospective demands. But it is not common to analyze water resource activity in terms of the character of decisions made and the strategies they reflect.

The theme of this volume is that by examining how people make their choices in managing water from place to place and time to time we can deepen our understanding of the process of water management, and thereby aid in finding more suitable ends and means of manipulating the natural water system. The first chapter outlines a framework in which a society's decisions as to water management may be examined. The following chapters discuss six of the major strategies which have been practiced in the United States. Much of the analysis draws upon personal experience with national and regional water planning efforts.

I am grateful to the committee on the William W. Cook Lectures on American Institutions at the University of Michigan at whose invitation this examination was presented as lectures and in seminars at the University. Dean Francis A. Allen of the Law School graciously made the arrangements. Professor Lyle E. Craine of the School of Natural Resources thoughtfully organized and led a faculty-student seminar in which a number of the ideas were reviewed. I owe much to all who took part in those and peripheral discussions, including the late Ayers Brinser, but I wish to thank especially William W. Bishop Jr., Charles Cooper, Samuel Dana, John J. Gannon, Spenser Havlick, Theodore Larsen, Joseph Sax, Gunther Schramm, Henry Vaux, and Walter J. Weber, Jr. for their suggestions.

James F. Johnson and Ian MacIver have assisted in preparing the materials. Robert D. Rugg drafted the diagrams.

I am indebted to Ian Burton, Wesley C. Calef, Lyle E. Craine, Irving K. Fox, John R. Hadd, Robert W. Kates, W. R. D. Sewell, and John R. Sheaffer for their comments on the manuscript.

The University of Chicago
July, 1968

Contents

Illustrations and Tables

A Progression
of Ends and Means

I

In their persistent efforts to come to terms with the uneven distribution of water in place and time across the plains and mountains of their continent, the American people have developed at least six major strategies. Although the earlier occupants canoed on streams, drew water from springs, and tended their maize in flooded washes largely in a spirit of man subject to the limits of nature, for the past 200 years the prevailing attitude has been one of man either conquering nature or living harmoniously with her. Whether as man the conqueror, or, at times unexpectedly, man the vanquished, or as man the cooperator he has dug several million wells, hacked out 12,000 miles of waterways, brought water to irrigate 30 million acres of land, and drained an even larger area. He has marshaled the water supply for his cities and 8,000 large industrial plants, curbed the frequency of overbank flows of several thousand streams, and harnessed more than 30,000,000 kilowatts of electric power capacity. In excess of 200 billion dollars at 1958 price levels has been invested in water development. Of this, about 20–30 percent has been spent under federal auspices.[1]

Now, near the peak of a massive construction program, a feeling is abroad that all is not well with the national water budget as modified by man. There is chronic and anxious talk of national water shortage. Eagerly, the results of experiments with giant nuclear reactors and desalting plants are awaited as offering sweeping remedies. Schemes for inter-basin transfer to Kansas from British Columbia and farther north which formerly were dismissed as grandiose are seriously proposed, albeit not by British Columbia. A new school of welfare economists has suggested instruments which throw into doubt the economic efficiency of public investment allocations for water development and offer more sophisticated measures. Public recognition of the mounting filth in streams and lakes has supported a huge program of waste treatment that barely keeps abreast of the growing flow of waste.

Although the agitation of 30 years ago for radical reorganization of federal water agencies along the lines of the Tennessee Valley Authority has been muffled, experimentation with new administrative forms is going forward in the Delaware Basin, in the regional commissions, and in the regional study initiatives established by the Water Resources Council. The pace of public education on water matters is stepping up, in no small measure under the gracious but not always gentle prodding of the League of Women Voters. Scholarly attempts are being made to breed a new type of scientist and administrator who can comprehend as well as cope with the complex of problems presented by water management, as witness the new graduate programs in water science and water management. The role of research as a tool for changing both comprehension and capability has received recognition and modest encouragement in the 51 new state water resources research centers. There is neither complacency nor warrant for it.

In this situation there are major opportunities to improve public management of water by making it less rigid and more responsive to accelerating technological change. The methods of allocating resources can be fashioned so as to increase efficiency by national standards as well as to be more sensitive to human needs for spiritual and aesthetic expression. The most menacing aspect of the prophecy that the United States is running out of water is that it may become self-fulfilling. For the view that water will be in short supply and requires augmentation sets in motion forces that in time worsen the situation. It is more likely that human welfare in the United States will be impaired through degradation of water quality or through inept management than from a physical scarcity of water.

Management of the resource is spread among a vast number of people—some private individuals, like the individual farmer who digs his own well, and some officers of federal and state agencies, like the Corps of Engineers which controls a network of navigation channels. Among them, they have altered the natural hydrologic cycle on a massive scale as shown in Figure I-1. Roughly two-thirds of the water which falls on the land of the United States as precipitation is returned to the atmosphere through evaporation and transpiration and is affected only by cropping practices which may change both flow and quality. Of that which remains, approximately one third is used directly in some fashion by man. Much of the unused flow is not available where it is wanted or when it is wanted. Except for the heavy consumptive use by irrigation lands, many of the uses, as in thermal power cooling, diminish the quantity hardly at all. It is their adverse alteration of temperature or chemical or bacteriological quality that impedes further use.

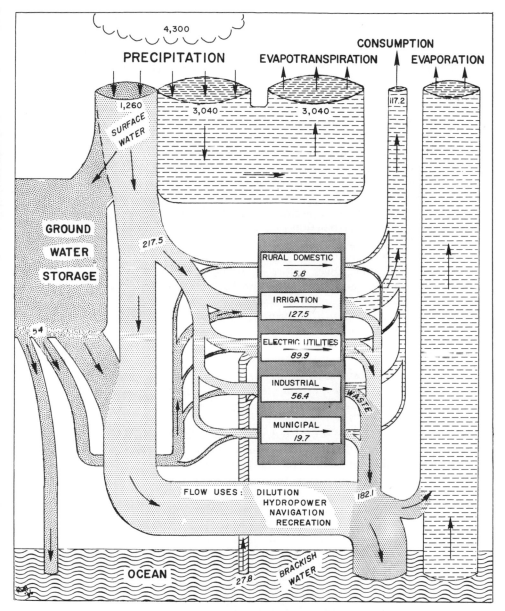

figures in billion gallons per day

Fig. I–1—Estimated Water Supply and Use in the United States, 1958. The calculations are rough at best but suggest the relative magnitude of different uses in the 48 states.

New Opportunities

In 1950 the President's Water Resources Policy Commission said,[2]

> . . . the Nation now is at a unique stage in water development. For
> several reasons, it is a stage which will never again recur.
>
> First, the Nation is on the threshold of a tremendous increase in
> the volume of construction for Federal water projects. The cost of
> projects now under construction or authorized is equal to the entire
> cost of all Federal projects heretofore constructed. And the projects
> planned but not authorized account for costs at least four times
> larger.
>
> Second, present mobilization plans impose heavy competing
> demands for construction materials, machinery, and men.
>
> Third, accumulated experience with basin wide programs in
> such diverse areas as the Columbia, the Missouri, and the Tennessee
> offers guidance never before available as to the wise planning of
> river development and as to the basic data essential to reaching
> sound decisions.
>
> Fourth, technical information on water, land, forest, and min-
> eral resources has accumulated rapidly in recent years. Much of this
> was not available to those who planned the authorized or proposed
> programs.
>
> Fifth, most basins are relatively undeveloped. Only a few key
> projects have been built or started. There is still time to make the
> necessary changes if it is decided that radical alterations are
> required.
>
> Once they are completed, major water control structures can be
> altered only with difficulty, or not at all. There are only a relatively
> few suitable dam sites, and once they are appropriated the possi-
> bilities for economic multiple-purpose development are very limited.
> Once an irrigation project is developed it cannot be moved because
> unfavorable soil or climatic factors are discovered. There is a sober-
> ing finality in the construction of a river basin development, and it
> behooves us to be sure we are right before we go ahead.

Fifteen years and 20 billion dollars later, a number of the major
basins in the United States have reached the point where the most
promising dam sites have been built, and a few are approaching the
situation where quantity of water now available from run-off within the
basin will be claimed in the foreseeable future. In the Tennessee virtually
complete regulation of the main stem of the channel has been achieved,
and storage has been completed on the Beech and two other tributaries.
These have been supplemented by investment in thermal generating
plants with a capacity of 12,000,000 kilowatts to supplement the installed
capacity of 3,000,000 kilowatts in the hydroelectric plants.[3] In the Mis-

souri basin, the chief dam sites along the main stem of the river above Omaha now are occupied by concrete and earth structures, and a large proportion of the storage in tributaries such as the Platte and Yellowstone has been claimed. With the completion of the Glen Canyon Dam, the storage capacity on the main stem of the Colorado and its lower tributaries outside of the controversial Grand Canyon reach will have been fully appropriated. Indeed, there is reason to think that the storage surfaces provided with the completion of additional dams will generate a total amount of evaporation in a year exceeding the incremental gain in storage resulting from recent construction.[4]

Figure I–2 shows the major drainage basins of the country classified according to relative degree of development of main-stem sites and of storage facilities, taking appropriation of main-stem reservoir sites and completion of tributary storage opportunities as the criteria. The Central Valley of California, the Colorado basin, the Rio Grande, and the major western tributaries of the Missouri as well as the Tennessee and Cumberland already have reached an advanced stage of development in terms of major storage opportunities.

In these circumstances it might be argued that certain major tasks of water management already have been achieved and that what remains is a relatively small supplement to the main-stem regulating works. The prevalence of this view that major channel and streamflow regulation constitutes the primary means and foundation of water management makes it all the more important to reassess the methods that have governed in the past and to examine the possibilities offered by new ones. For reasons which will be advanced in later chapters, the prevailing methods are ill-suited to the changing conditions of both the supply and its use. A vast arena for water management of other types remains available to man on the North American continent.

In addition to possible improvement in handling water in the United States, it seems likely that in two other directions useful lessons could be drawn from the water experience. One is in application of these lessons to developing areas overseas. The second has to do with methods for comprehensive management of resources in urban areas.

Over the years the United States has imported highly useful techniques from overseas, including some of those for water and waste treatment, and basic concepts such as forest-runoff relations. It continues to gain from other nations, but it now is exporting its own water skills to developing countries on a broad scale. Since its dam design and construction methods were transferred by Cooper and his associates to the Dnieper in the 1930's, its techniques have been spread through the activities of the Bureau of Reclamation, university centers, construction com-

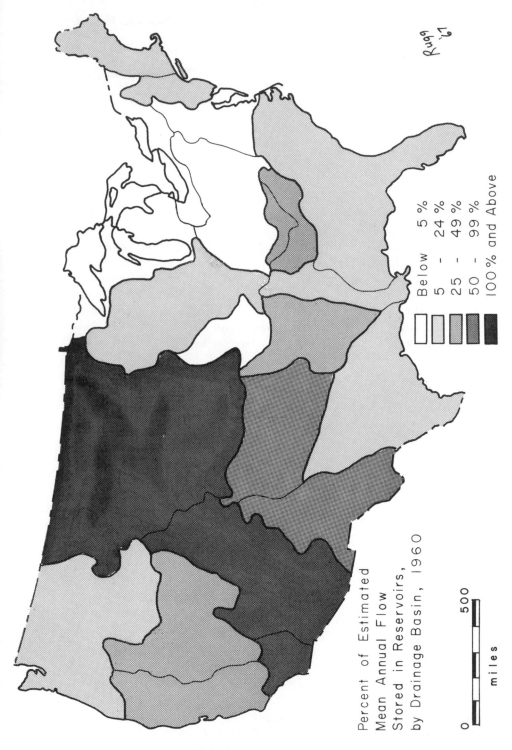

Percent of Estimated
Mean Annual Flow
Stored in Reservoirs,
by Drainage Basin, 1960

Below   5 %
5 - 24 %
25 - 49 %
50 - 99 %
100 % and Above

miles

0   500

Rugg
'67

Fig. I-2a—Stream Flow Storage, 1960. Estimates are for entire basins and do not show differences among subbasins.

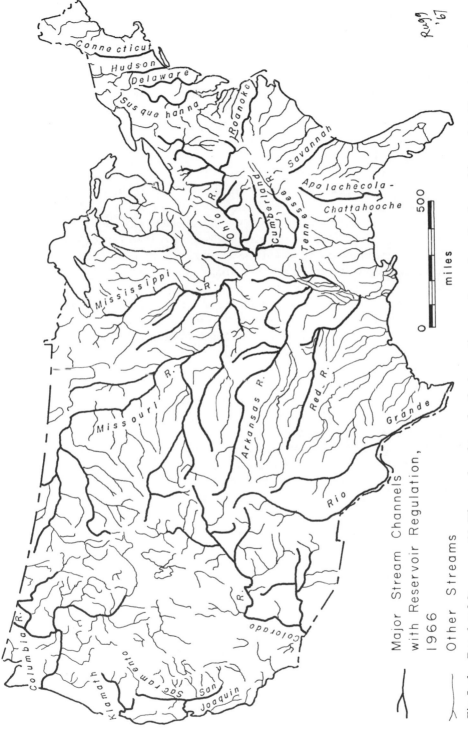

Rugg '67

Major Stream Channels
with Reservoir Regulation,
1966

Other Streams

Fig. I–2b—Regulated Streams, 1966. The reaches shown by the heavy line are those where the channel is regulated by storage improvement works on the main stream or on principal tributaries.

panies, and consulting engineers. Bilateral aid programs have enforced the diffusion process. In its proposal for a Water for Peace program, as announced by President Johnson on September 3, 1966, the United States appeared to be seeking in a more explicit way to dominate the style of thinking about water management in other countries. In moving ahead with a so-called international conference without adequate discussion with countries concerned and without directly involving the international agencies responsible for continuing cooperation, the United States not only weakened the United Nations structure but increased the risk of impeding rather than enhancing the management of water in developing countries. Such countries with their limited stocks of capital and trained personnel can ill afford the luxury of inefficient investment in river regulation. To the extent, then, that methods lead to projects which pay only modest returns or are net drains on the national income, as with many American water projects, their transfer is a disservice. A dam yielding minimal returns which would receive only scant notice in a country where tobacco sales are 60 times the total budget of the United Nations might spell disaster in a country where it is the chief public works investment. An assessment of domestic experience with water may help judge its suitability for other peoples, lands, climates, and economies.

Even if it were not pressing to appraise American experience in the interest of improving water management at home and overseas, it would be peculiarly relevant to public efforts at managing land and air in metropolitan areas, for water is the most visible of all resources systems. It is the first to have undergone public management on a large scale, and it is the first where man has attempted to cope in a rigorous way with integrated management of linked resources in the same area. Although foresters have attempted to design multiple-purpose management plans for all of the physical resources in smaller areas, it is in water that man has made his most ambitious efforts to deal with the whole complex network of transformation of landscape in the human interest. And it is in the sprawl of metropolitan areas that similar attempts increasingly receive their most exacting tests. Questions of multiple-purpose planning, agency coordination, economic evaluation, and standards of public preferences were confronted earlier and concretely in drainage basin management. Some of the lessons promise to be applicable to urban design and programs.

The Nature of the Decisions

A convenient and instructive way of assessing the water record is to ask what is the nature of the decisions which have been made in water management. If the American people are thought of as being engaged in a game with a bounteous and capricious nature, then their methods of responding to natural diversity and fluctuations in the water resource in seeking to fulfill their aims may be seen as strategies. By strategy is meant a distinctive combination of aim, means, and decision criteria. Defining the strategies which have prevailed and now dominate American water planning activity calls for examination of the distinguishing aims, methods, and decision criteria applied by the managers who have been responsible for the resource decisions over the years. Neither aims nor means may be regarded as fixed. The United States has had and continues to entertain a variety of aims and of means of reaching them in its transactions with the environment. At no time has there been one strategy alone. Strategies have evolved and overlapped. Each displays a special association of aims, methods, and criteria.

Analysis of the character of the decisions made by water managers is essential to an understanding of why there are chronic discrepancies between the hopes and the accomplishments of water planners. The question of why federal efforts to reduce flood losses did not have their desired effect suggests that it is important to look into the ways in which people who made decisions about water management did so, and how that behavior varied from one part of the floodplain to another. Over the years the United States has been quick and energetic in making studies leading to normative judgments or to plans for water development but has been extremely slow, indeed reluctant, to make any appraisal of what has happened after a project is constructed and put into operation.

The course of events of water management overseas as well as in the United States indicates that the most important single factor clouding the horizon is the broadening gap between the level of scientific and technological knowledge and its sensitive application in daily practice. Irrigators fail to use water-saving devices, industrial managers ignore improved means of water processing. If the gap is to be narrowed, there will need to be deeper appreciation of those conditions of decisions which now impede the adoption of new practices.

In asking what characteristics of decision making constitute the past and prevailing strategies of water management, the crucial process of decision may be approached by a variety of paths. One is the traditional engineering approach in which river basin management is seen as the design of suitable physical works. The common test of efficacy is in its use of water, soil, concrete, and steel so as to achieve desired regulation with minimum inputs of materials. The common criteria are safety, workability, durability, and economy.

The engineering approach has been greatly modified by economic analysis which beginning in the middle 1950's pointed to methods of optimization in allocation of resources. From this standpoint the design of water systems looks to determining what combinations of type and scale of works would be most efficient in terms of marginal returns. Choices are seen as approaching or departing from the optimal solution.

At the same time there has been a long series of analyses by political scientists and public administrators of the conditions in which public agencies organize to carry out water planning. As demonstrated in the works of Maass, McKinley, Pealy, and others,[5] the focus has been on the character of administrative organization and its relation to political process. Decisions are examined with a view to finding the political forces that shape them, or the influence of particular structures, such as an inter-agency committee, upon the outcome.

Another approach is that provided by sociologists seeking to examine community organization and process relating to the formation and support of agencies making decisions about water management. The work of Firey, Selznik, and Simon[6] has been highly suggestive in showing the role of agency identity in shaping choices and the ways in which sub-optimal choices are preferred.

Although it might be expected that from the field of ecology would come grounds for critical analysis, those who pursue the grail of understanding the complex ecological web involved in changing the hydrologic cycle have been so few in number and so limited in scientific opportunities that little in the way of broad appraisal has thus far resulted. They have asked disturbing and fundamental questions revealing the state of ignorance as to what the consequences of new construction may be for plants, animals, and man himself, but have not been able to provide satisfying answers.

The analysis offered in this book adopts a somewhat different model of decision making. In it economic optimization is regarded as one of the factors affecting decisions but as having in common with estimates of the water resource and recognition of available technology and spatial linkages a role which is highly conditioned by the perception which individual managers have of those factors. Social institutions are seen as affecting both perception and the freedom or incentive which individuals have to operate. Perception of (1) range of choice, (2) water resource, (3) technology, (4) economic efficiency, and (5) spatial linkages are the chief components, each influenced by social institutions. The distinctive aspects of the model are that it makes economic optimization only one of five factors involved in decision making, and that all five factors are seen

as being profoundly influenced by the culture of the area and as manipulated by the organization and character of social guides.

Using this framework, it will be helpful to assess strategies of management according to three basic characteristics.

First, the immediate purposes sought may be distinguished according to whether they are single or multiple. This is a traditional distinction between the single-purpose dam for flood control, irrigation, or
power, and the multiple-purpose dam, serving two or more purposes,
which played such an influential role in the development of river basin
programs in the 1930's and 1940's. In a broader sense, the long-term aims
of water management are mixed and ambiguous in most instances, but
the immediate, narrow purposes can be defined more readily.

Second, the means employed to achieve aims may be distinguished
according to whether the planning considers only one class of means or
reviews a broader range of possible techniques. The distinction here is
between consideration of single types of engineering construction, crop
control, or land regulation, and consideration of the relative advantages
and disadvantages of two or more of these types of activity.

Third, the responsible management agencies may be divided into
those which are predominantly private and those which are predominantly public, recognizing that there is, inevitably, a division of public
and private responsibility along a gradual spectrum. Thus, a watershed
protection project of the Soil Conservation Service may be partly public
and partly private. Indeed, there are today only a very few water management undertakings which are exclusively private. On the other hand,
if the management process is regarded as comprising, according to our
definition, the full social action of managing a resource, there are likewise few water projects which are exclusively public in character. For
example, the federally maintained navigation channels serve their full
function only through the operation of privately owned barge lines.
Whether private or public, similar groups of individuals or organization
managers seem to use somewhat similar criteria for decision.

Other characteristics of the decision may be highly significant. The
time horizon of private investors can be contrasted with the long-term
investment period of a few private developers and of the predominant
group of government agencies which use horizons of 50 to 100 years in
drawing up basin plans. The spatial distribution of benefits and costs
may be examined. They may be divided into those which focus on local
benefits and costs attaching directly to an area in the neighborhood of
the water management operation, such as the cost to a town of taking
water supply out of a nearby stream; and those of a regional character,

such as the cost to a town which in withdrawing water supply considers the effect of its withdrawal upon the use of the stream in a lower part of the drainage area.

The character of risk-taking can be examined according to the way in which managers discount risk and the degree of provision they make for dealing with the uncertainty of natural occurrences and human action. According to these two criteria, the management decisions can be grouped into one of four classes as noted in the following table in which risk is related to preparations to deal with uncertainty. For convenience, risk may be divided into that which is undertaken with a discount rate approximate to the mortgage rate and that which has a lower rate representing some degree of public intervention in the assumption of risk.

TABLE I–1

CLASSES OF ADJUSTMENT TO RISK AND UNCERTAINTY
IN WATER MANAGEMENT

Risk discounted at:	Preparation for uncertainty	
	Dislocations expected	Dislocations minimized
Current mortage rates	Private irrigation Municipal sewerage Private water supply	Municipal water supply Private power generation
Lesser rates supported by public agencies	Public rural flood protection Watershed protection	Public irrigation Public urban flood protection Public navigation

Uncertainty may be divided into (1) those preparations which assume that the operator—whether private or public—will from time to time suffer major dislocations due to the occurrence of a natural phenomenon, as in the case of private investments in small agricultural farm levees or in the drilling by townspeople of wells which may go dry in a rare drought of long duration, and (2) those in which the planning assumes that the works will have to deal with the maximum contingencies which are anticipated. Thus, most of the public irrigation projects are intended to provide water in all years, including years of severe drought; private power developments seek to minimize power failures; and most urban flood control projects are intended to care for some limit short of the maximum probable flood. To be sure, the Corps of Engineers in its estimates of the "standard project flood" specifically includes the possibility that larger floods may be experienced, but in its design of spillway and other emergency features and in its economic analysis it generally seeks to deal with the maximum reasonable occurrence, and while the works may not be intended to provide full protection against the extremely rare event, in contrast to protection works for farm lands, they are intended to withstand it without conspicuous failure. There is inevitable ambiguity in the distinction between uncertainty and risk. The decision to provide against the drought of least expectancy is in part a matter of risk taking, but it also is a matter of guarding against the unexpected event whenever it may occur.

Six Types of Strategy

If the sweep of water management is examined in the light of purpose, means, and management agency, six types of strategy stand out. The simplest and most widespread is single-purpose construction by private managers as exemplified by farm water supply. Similar to it but significantly different in decision criteria is single-purpose construction by public managers of which the oldest is navigation. Third and now most prominent in the public mind is multiple-purpose construction by public managers. Less well developed is single-purpose action by public agencies using multiple means, illustrated by flood loss reduction. When the means are enlarged to include research as a conscious management tool, as in the case of weather modification, a fifth strategy emerges. Finally, a merging of multiple purposes and multiple means, including research, gives a strategy which is not yet clearly formed but toward which there is groping on several fronts, particularly in metropolitan areas.

Other construction strategies are practiced, as illustrated by the limited effort at multiple-purpose management by a private agency on the Wisconsin River, but they are not as widespread or as persistent as those described. Strategies of public regulation are in operation, as in state permits for waste disposal and in federal licensing of power sites, but they have not been as influential. Many others would be possible with sufficient modification of social institutions. Within each major class are striking differences, chiefly according to the decision criteria. The effect of appraising water management under these particular categories is to direct attention to similarities and differences in the nature of decision making.

Three types of questions may be addressed to each strategy. The initial question relates to how decisions are made. Who makes what choices? The other two questions relate to the consequences of the choice. What is the effect upon the public welfare? What is the effect upon the natural environment? The second and third are linked, for any modification of the natural environment has significance in the public welfare, but inasmuch as those linkages often are difficult to trace it may be helpful to try to separate them in the inquiry.

There are no fully adequate answers to any one of those questions. This is partly because the analytical methods to determine effects, as in the case of income redistribution from building an irrigation scheme or impacts upon ecosystems from a new reservoir, are still so imperfect. It is partly because few attempts have been made to apply what methods are available to the appraisal of completed works. The shelves are bursting with plans and with normative studies of optimal solutions. A few inches will suffice to record what is known, in fact, to have happened. The emphasis has been on plans rather than performance. What follows is largely speculative and is drawn from scraps of evidence. It may prove useful if it stirs investigation of the record rather than the dreams of American water management.

Single-Purpose Construction: Rural Water Supply and Navigation

II

Man's one omnipresent need for water is domestic. Where people live in communities in the United States they typically satisfy their household demands through some sort of community water supply, often inconspicuous, in which responsibility for choice, treatment, and distribution of water is vested either in a public agency or in a private agency acting under franchise. Where individuals in rural areas or on urban peripheries must shift for themselves in obtaining water they usually carry the full responsibility for developing their own supply.

Navigation improvement typically is carried out at public expense and in recent years, almost wholly under one federal agency, the Corps of Engineers. Rural water supply and navigation thus represent two extremes of management, the farmer and suburbanite being largely on their own and the water transport improvement being under a central planning and construction organization that cooperates with local governments. They have the common characteristics of serving a single aim by a single means and of relying on construction as that means. In these respects they are like the efforts made until early in the twentieth century to develop agricultural drainage, hydroelectric power, irrigation, municipal water supply, and waste disposal.

Single-purpose construction is the oldest of water management strategies and still the most widespread. The long and contrasting experience with private construction of rural water supplies and federal construction of navigation improvement illustrates some elementary aspects of decision making and indicates how social guides may affect them over time and space. Without attempting a description of the works which have been constructed, a few generalities can be drawn from the available data as to how the management decisions have been made and as to their consequences for Americans and their continent. Brief mention is made of other single-purpose construction. In each, attention is directed to the way in which managers perceive their choices, the resource, the available technology, the economic efficiency, and linkages with others, to the guides exercised by society, and to the likely effects upon landscape and society. Because the conclusions are drawn chiefly from reconnaissance and a few detailed studies, they are tentative and are subject to revision as more intensive appraisals are made.

Every Man for Himself

In many parts of the country the farmer or the suburb dweller who wants to develop a new water supply or supplement his present supply appears to consider a wide range of sources from which he might draw: he may look to streams if there be such, to wells reaching underground sources, to water stored on the surface in ponds or reservoirs, and to the flow of rain off his roof. In part, he adopts this breadth of view from the American Indians who used a wide set of sources but did not sense the full availability of waters from aquifers. In part, he inherits views of water availability from European experience, as in the Southwest where greater emphasis was placed upon the possibility of collecting water off roofs in cisterns than in Eastern humid areas. The mix of choices which he canvasses still differs from one section of the country to another but no major opportunities are ignored over large areas.

In estimating the resources available to him, he gradually has become aware of the availability of the underground sources and is prepared to pump from depths of several hundred feet, and typically seems to look at water sources first in terms of whether there will be sufficient quantity to meet year-round demands.[1] There is little current interest in sources such as cisterns or ephemeral streams which would yield only seasonally or which would have such low yields that they would need to be supplemented at other times. For quality, he appears to look for water which satisfies certain minimum standards of taste, odor, and bacteriological composition. Taste standards are reported to differ greatly from one part of the United States to another according to the natural mineralization of surface waters, with other limits set by the customary load. The housewife increasingly imposes higher requirements for water that will not stain clothing or impede dish washing. Often these can be met either by finding better sources or by water softening, and the latter is more common.

The bacteriological and mineral standards for public supplies have been formalized by state health departments over the years but in the process an interesting shift in emphasis took place. Whereas in the nineteenth century great stress was laid by individual water users upon the chemical quality of the water as they perceived it,[2] today the individual water user thinks primarily in terms of whether or not it meets the minimum bacteriological standards and the dictates of convenience and sightliness in washing clothes. The emphasis by both Indians and early settlers upon what were regarded as the peculiar medicinal qualities of natural springs, a discrimination which in the 1800's led to long migrations or vacation journeys by those who could afford them, was largely abandoned. Today, the water user is concerned chiefly with preventing transmission of intestinal disease and with avoiding hardness which causes special problems in laundry and household cleaning. The change in emphasis has tended to obscure the importance of other attributes even though there is a rising body of scientific information to suggest that minor differences in water softness or in the content of trace elements may bear a significant relation to health. The common view of underground water as being inherently purer than surface water prevails even when the detergents from a neighbor's septic tank make suds at the faucet.

There has been a wide and rapid diffusion of technology for extracting water, the most notable being in well-drilling apparatus and in pumps for raising water and maintaining system pressure. The home owner in most parts of the United States seems to be aware of means for drilling a well or pumping water from great depths, and the possibilities of surface storage are understood where soil conservation districts are active. Although relatively cheap facilities are available for collecting water from roofs and storing it in sanitary tanks, they are not widely recognized, and the technology of transporting water from a distant source is known chiefly in areas with acute limits on supply. In general, domestic supplies are especially difficult to obtain in three types of areas. In extremely arid zones where potable water is not naturally present, as in parts of the Mohave Desert, the only choice is transport. Where surface supplies are meager and ground water is available only at great depths, reliance must be placed on submersible pumps. Where the surface supplies are scarce and ground waters are highly mineralized, the choice is between transport or local treatment. In Figure II–1 the major problem areas are defined as those with less than 10 inches mean annual run-off and with conditions of depth or mineral content of ground water that require heavy technological inputs to make it usable.

In installing water supplies the American farmer and suburbanite seem satisfied with water systems which will give them needed amounts for the year without high risk of failure. Within very broad limits set by income, there has been little discriminating judgment between alternate sources according to relative cost, behavior that is similar to the observed inelastic demand for water from piped supplies in urban areas. A farmer

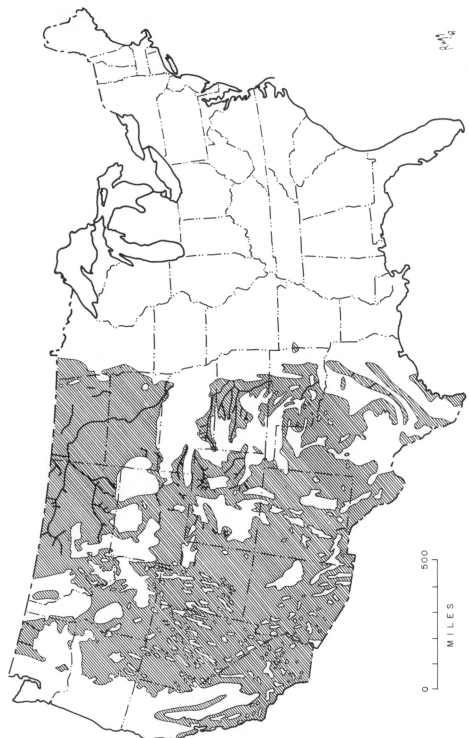

Fig. II-1—Problem Areas for Rural Domestic Water Supply. Major problem areas for rural water supply are delimited first by excluding all land having 10 or more inches of mean annual runoff. The remaining areas are excluded if they have potable supplies readily available in valley sediments or in aquifers. (From maps of runoff and from Thomas, *op.cit.*)

MILES

0   500

will put down a well for convenience purposes even though it might be cheaper to collect the same amount of water from his roofs, thus placing a high value on convenience. And an exurbanite will tend, according to scattered observations, to select whatever system within some range of capital cost promises the least complicated method of operation and maintenance. To some degree, the manager is influenced by information from equipment salesmen. However, when the homeowner considers adding storage for fire-fighting purposes and thereby reduces fire insurance premiums, as in building farm ponds, he appears to compare expected costs and benefits more closely.

In making installations, the owners characteristically ignore the effects of their action upon people elsewhere. Even in suburban areas where new houseowners find themselves pumping detergent-laden effluent, the tendency is to avoid confrontation in recovering damage or restricting new building. The prevailing view appears to be that each man should be free to shift for himself in obtaining water for home use and should have little regard for the consequences for others who in turn will shift for themselves in drawing from stream or aquifer.

Against the background of this very broad description of the ways in which individual water supplies now are obtained in the United States, it may be asked what social action has assisted or constrained the resulting water development. It is remarkable that government agencies do relatively little to assist the individual houseowner in making decisions about water supply. The chief contribution has been through federal and state geological studies of availability of ground water. These, however, are carried out chiefly to assist communities in search of ground water or to aid farmers looking for irrigation water supplies. The hydrologic studies of surface water by the U.S. Geological Survey and the Soil Conservation Service are aimed more at identifying the effects of land management or the possibilities for large-scale water improvement than at assembling data and information on relationships which would enable individual users to design their own systems. Nor are governments particularly active in spreading understanding of new technologies. State health agencies give advice as to means of maintaining the safety of water from a health standpoint, and the agricultural extension services carry out a small amount of research and distribute some information on methods of well, cistern, and dam construction. This is principally through the medium of information bulletins, and the amount of direct technical advice is minimal. Not until recent years have the governments given any substantial aid in the financing of new water installations. Since 1961, under the association loan system of the Farmers' Home

Administration, about 100,000 farm families have been served by new common water facilities. Mortgage insurance provisions of the Federal Housing Administration and the Veterans Administration underwrite new water systems as part of residential construction, and specify minimum plumbing and reliable sources.

At the same time, government intervenes in only a few instances in development of new supplies. Both federal and state legislatures ignored the strenuous advice of Powell that the surface water of the semi-arid and arid zones should be carefully husbanded. He wanted a system of land and water use based on water sources the right to which would attach to the land.[3] State water rights legislation gives first priority to domestic water use, and exercises virtually no control over individual withdrawals of water so long as they are primarily for domestic purposes rather than irrigation and so long as the right is employed. Thus, among the fifty states only three make any strenuous effort to control the drilling of new wells or the extraction of water for domestic purposes. When Colorado tried in 1965 to license the drilling of new wells for farmsteads and homesteads it found itself impaled on opposition by the general public.[4]

In passing on plans for new residential construction, county and local health officers certify that the arrangements for waste disposal are sufficient to permit safe farm or suburban water supplies. The water installations themselves are not subject to rigorous inspection and regulation.

The fact is that private entrepreneurs play the major role in giving assistance to individuals who wish to develop their own water supplies. In estimating resources the water diviners have been far more popular than the geologists, partly because they are more readily available, partly because they deal directly and satisfactorily in the public mind with the complex questions and ambiguity that surround the understanding of invisible underground water supplies, and partly because they function on a man-to-man basis without public intermediary. It is interesting that in this most ubiquitous of resource decisions, reliance upon witchcraft is larger among the United States population than in any other sector of individual resource management. Although no careful studies have been made of water-witching beyond Vogt and Hyman's in the Colorado Plateau of New Mexico, it clearly is widespread and accepted.[5] There still is no scientific evidence that the diviners have a degree of accuracy exceeding random chance, but the proportion of the population that tends to rely on the diviner is probably of the same magnitude as that which looks to patent medicines in preference to the trained physician in dealing with minor ailments, or to astrology for daily guidance.

Well drillers, builders, and manufacturers of pumps, tanks, filters, and plumbing equipment continue to be major carriers of innovation. The Aerometer Company with its windwills and tanks had a profound effect on the occupancy of the Great Plains. Much of the urban residential invasion of isolated rural lands and of desert territory in Arizona and California is dependent upon private enterprise either in finding underground water or obtaining reliable water hauling.

Lack of government assistance and intervention has not appeared to curb economic development or cause serious maladjustments in social welfare or environment. It is doubtful that in any of the water problem areas the lack of water for domestic purposes has been a major obstacle to development of soil and timber resources. The farmer who is forced to haul water twenty miles in times of drought in the drier sections of the High Plains may be subject to inconvenience and some additional cost but is not prevented effectively from tilling the soil for his bumper crop of wheat in the less frequent good year. There are exceptional cases such as in areas with highly mineralized ground supplies. These are few in number and restricted in extent. During the great drought of 1934–36 many farmers suffered water shortage but neither then nor in subsequent years of drought did domestic shortage seem to be directly related to a change in land use or redistribution of population.

But has the way in which domestic water has been developed basically altered the natural resource to which it is related? Clearly it has done so in a few areas where individuals have made heavy drafts upon limited groundwater supplies, chiefly surficial supplies. One of the great areas of individual exhaustion of deeper aquifers is in the Dakota sandstone of the eastern Dakotas, where relatively effective state regulation in the 1920's served to curb the withdrawal to the estimated volume of input in the replenishment areas of the Black Hills. A few other instances may be noted in which aquifers have been drawn down by domestic use, in contrast to irrigation and municipal withdrawals. Apparently there have been no serious modifications in soil or surface stream networks through domestic water withdrawals: the amounts are small and the users dispersed.

To sum up, individual water supplies are managed with virtually no public investment; little public research directed to improving the process of choice; sparse technical service; and heavy reliance upon private agencies, chiefly diviners, well drillers, and equipment manufacturers, to give required information. The chief public constraint is that of safeguarding health by regulating waste fields and plumbing. The consequences of the strategy are difficult to assess in terms of economic development. Its effects upon environment are localized. While there is no evidence that the economic growth of any region yet has suffered seriously from lack of domestic water supply, underground supplies have been impaired drastically in some areas. The strategy of relying upon single-purpose construction by private managers also has nurtured public attitudes that water is a good without price and that it is a private property. These have severely handicapped later community efforts to manage water for other purposes by supporting the view that water should be distributed at minimal price and that public agencies have an obligation to do so.

Every Power Company for Itself

The other major application of single-purpose private construction has been in generating hydroelectric power. Private corporations and a few municipalities pioneered in power generation, building on the precedent of the wheels which provided mechanical power to mills until electricity supplanted them in the early 1900's. Although Bureau of Reclamation projects began to incorporate hydroelectric generating equipment at storage projects after 1906, the companies had the field largely to themselves until the mid 1930's; since then they have been in guerrilla competition with public agencies, and now account for more than 85 percent of total installed generating capacity and for about half of all hydroelectric capacity.

Typically, private developers canvass hydro sites along with thermal opportunities and measure available stream flow with prudence.[6] They experiment with new technology for thermal generation, water storage (pumped storage schemes were soon tried in the private sector), and for energy transmission, maintaining some common research facilities. Their economic analysis hinges on expected net returns and lays only incidental weight on indirect social effects while seeking to forecast market response to price changes. Transmission grids are interlocked on a national scale, and while the struggle for acquisitions through corporate mergers has been strenuous, direct territorial competition is slight because of state and municipal franchise arrangements.

Federal regulation under the Federal Water Power Act governs the right to build dams across navigable waterways and their tributaries and to construct interstate transmission lines; state utility commissions regulate rates and market areas. One of the principal justifications given for federal construction of hydro plants under the New Deal was that state regulation had broken down, permitting monopoly practices. It was claimed that the only effective ways to stimulate lower pricing and expansion of markets to unserved consumers were to establish competitive federal producers and to support competitive municipal and cooperative distributors through preference clauses and the Rural Electrification Administration.[7] Under that pressure, private rates were lowered and marketing activities were enhanced, but what constitutes a fair federal yardstick has been debated ever since.

Inasmuch as the earlier and most readily developed sites required little storage and the companies had no way of charging for nonreimbursable navigation and flood control benefits, their projects tended to make minimal alterations in landscape. When faced with possible interference with wildlife or recreation, they either bought control or kept clear, but they early saw the opportunities for water-based recreation at a few reservoirs such as Lake of the Ozarks. How far their pricing and marketing policies encumbered rather than advanced economic growth is difficult to say. Certainly the threat of federal intervention spurred basic changes over a decade and still does so.

Private hydro development has shown openness to considering production alternatives, realism in gauging the resource, and ingenuity in devising new technology. With the support of often short-sighted state control and under the curb of dealing only in vendible products, it has shown insensitivity to broader social considerations.

Farmers and Manufacturers for Themselves

Land drainage and irrigation are management practices which have shifted from private to public responsibility and then in recent years have shown a renewal of individual farmer action. Much of the drainage which made parts of the Atlantic Coastal Plain and the wet lands of northern Ohio and Indiana habitable was undertaken by individual farmers. As they found it necessary to band together in drainage districts, they worked with county or state assessment authority.

A large part of the more than 130,000,000 acres of drained land has been developed by individual farmers. Their perception of the opportunities for drainage in relation to the resources of soil and water seems to vary greatly within communities, although they are relatively quick to use new techniques for drainage such as mechanical ditchers, tile layers, and moles. The record suggests that they tend to judge investment by short-term returns in comparison with other possible inputs, to underestimate the immediate costs, and to disregard the consequences for their neighbors downstream.[8] Beyond technical advice on soils and tiling and ditching methods from agricultural extension services, they receive advice from manufacturers and the technicians of the Department of Agriculture who help them qualify for agricultural conservation payments or who design the restoration of drained areas for propagation of waterfowl. The drainage districts have relied chiefly on private engineers and have a long record of getting into trouble through neglected maintenance or the underestimate of water disposal problems.

Never regarded as a primary federal responsibility, although recognized as a project purpose in the Flood Control Act of 1944, land drainage claims the interests of agricultural, mosquito eradication, wildlife, and flood control agencies; and it was recognition of conflict over the social wisdom of new drainage undertakings while wildlife interests were trying to restore nesting and feeding areas for migratory waterfowl which led to the first federal coordination of water plans. Its effects upon ecosystems through destruction of wetlands are massive, and it has been essential to the farming use of large sectors of the country.

Somewhat similar observations apply to irrigation during its earlier days when it was carried out in arid lands by individual farmers, water companies, or local districts.[9] Its present characteristics are mentioned under the heading of single-purpose public construction.

Finally, the heavy use of American streams by industry for water supply and waste disposal should be noted albeit briefly. Supply and disposal can be linked as they are in management decisions. Judging from limited studies, industrial managers seem to consider a wide range of choices in both supply and waste disposal.[10] They are moderately aware of differences in water quality and volume and of techniques for treatment. Their economic consideration of water supply is minimal, but much more attention is given to the costs of waste disposal. Responsive to public opinion and the threat of government regulation, they canvass means of satisfying those public standards. With public policies of providing water at low cost, management seems to move toward more intense control chiefly to maintain quality or avoid inconvenience. In the lack of clear definition of public preferences as to stream cleanliness, they tend to let the effluent reach the limit unless there are gains from waste recovery.

The Corps of Engineers for Columbus River

The approach of the American people to the development of their natural waterways was caught by Mark Twain and Charles Warner in *The Gilded Age* when they had the eager young engineer take the visitor out to the banks of the local stream, locally known as Goose Run but recently endowed with the name of the Columbus River. With a glow in his eye the engineer says, "The Columbus River, if deepened, and widened, and straightened, and made a little longer, would be one of the greatest rivers in our western country." This belief that with enough manipulation any creek could become a major artery of commerce and culture has motivated investment in water improvement since the early canal-building period. That it has done so in the face of a record of mixed success and failure remains one of the interesting enigmas of American water development. The aims never have been clear; national efficiency usually has been mixed with local aspiration in promoting new projects.

The Great Lakes improvements and chief ocean harbors are omitted from the class of waterway development discussed here. They compose a major system linked with ocean transport, having their own characteristics of carrier and traffic, and, with the exception of the St. Lawrence power installations and a few other ties, are not strongly related to inland improvements. The Great Lakes account for about 7 percent of total domestic freight traffic, and the inland waterways for more than 9 percent.

Today, the system of making decisions about improvements in inland waterways is one in which a narrow range of choice is considered. Project plans are prepared by the Corps of Engineers in response to Congressional resolutions, submitted to the Congress, and, if authorized, built and maintained by the Corps with whatever local contributions may be required. A proposed improvement is appraised by estimating the traffic which would move, and computing prospective gains and losses. If it can be shown, by whatever system of economic calculation is involved, to promise an excess of benefits over costs, using the prevailing freight rates, it is recommended for construction.

Essentially, the choices are (1) to continue with present rail, highway, and waterway facilities at prevailing rates, (2) build the new waterway and divert part of the existing or prospective traffic from other carriers, or (3) build the waterway and readjust the rates on the competing carriers to the lower level set by the waterway costs so that while traffic movements may not change, the charges to shippers will decrease proportionally. The third case is reminiscent of Charles Lamb's arrival at roast pig by burning the entire house: construction investment in the waterway is sacrificed in order to obtain a change in freight rates. Local interests insist that the Interstate Commerce Commission regulatory processes are so unresponsive that this is the only effective course and that they stand to gain in any event from the expenditures for construction. The Corps at times has pointed out the illogic of building new waterways to regulate rail rates, but anyhow Congressional precedent and policy limits the Corps' exploration of choices rather rigidly to the first two.

The amount of water available for navigation improvements is calculated with caution. Natural channels are mapped meticulously. Stream discharge and elevation measurements commonly are available for the larger streams on which navigation is contemplated, and are made where required. Any Goose Run is considered possibly capable of transformation into a mighty Columbus River.

In this same spirit the technology of water transportation improvement is seen primarily as changing river channel and flow, and secondarily as modifying the means of transport. The Corps' most substantial venture into research is the Waterways Experiment Station which in response to pressure from civil engineers took on pioneering work in hydraulic models as a basis for both navigation and flood control designs. It has paid some attention to port facilities and less to vessels. Except for research on barge design under the Inland Waterways Corporation when it was operating to attempt to build water traffic, the chief improvements in barges and tows have come from the bulk carriers, principally of petroleum and coal, and from the Tennessee Valley Authority. Between 1940 and the 1960's the power of towboats increased almost ten-fold, and the barge capacity grew even more, particularly for tankers.

As already indicated, economic efficiency is judged by benefit-cost analysis and is seen from two different vantage points. The Corps seeks to compute national costs and benefits, and to allocate a portion of the costs to local interests where the benefits would accrue principally to one shipper. Local groups gauge the importance of the proposal in terms of construction expenditures, savings to shippers, and the anticipated multiplier effects on industrial and commercial activity. The final arbiter, Congress, insists on favorable benefit-cost rates and is sensitive to the local preferences.

Some attention is given to the linkage of waterway improvements to economic activity in other areas, as when the issue of the St. Lawrence deepening was opposed by New York interests seeing it as a threat to barge traffic down the Hudson. The Great Lakes improvements have received attention as a system.[11] The effects of waterway development on growth have been explored in the Tennessee Basin.[12] In general, however, the broader regional effects are not studied explicitly.

The effects of navigation construction on other aspects of the environment tend to draw special investigation only in the case of large projects. On the main stem of the Mississippi they are, of course, monumental: the whole channel above the Missouri to St. Paul is converted into reservoirs; the reach from Cairo to below New Orleans is shortened by cutoffs and curbed by revetments so that channel characteristics are modified drastically. On the Ohio the low navigation structures have had far less effect on environment than the huge storage reservoirs in the tributaries, including the multiple-purpose reservoirs along the whole length of the Tennessee. The larger alterations have come with departures from single purpose. The Delaware Ship Canal and the Florida Ship Canal projects inspired persistent efforts on the part of certain local interests to explore the probable impacts of canal construction upon the ground water resources of adjoining areas. Others preferred to ignore such consequences, and the same attitude continued into the presidential election of 1964 when a group of distinguished citizens proposed nuclear construction of a rectangular network of waterways across the country with blithe disregard for the effects upon natural stream patterns and ecosystems. The Upper Mississippi Waterway plans were seen as linked with a significant international waterfowl flyway, but the prevailing approach to small streams has been single purpose.

The prevailing social guides to waterway development are threefold. Federal powers are exercised by the Corps to investigate, construct, and maintain waterways. Licensing is used to prevent undue encroachments on channels or interference with stream flow, both by Corps of Engineers regulations and by Federal Power Commission permits for new power generating structures. Common carriers on water and land are subject to Interstate Commerce Commission rate regulation but the private carriers who account for the bulk of inland water borne traffic need only meet safety requirements.

Goodrich and his colleagues have shown that the early history of canal building by state governments, following on a few small ventures by private investors, was in facilities which offered substantial returns to the economy, particularly in stimulating interregional trade through drastic reductions in freight charges by comparison with wagon transport.[13] During the three cycles of building between 1815 and 1860, about four-fifths of the investment yielded direct benefits exceeding direct costs. A few of the canals failed to achieve their desired aims. Indeed, some of them were obsolete before or shortly after their completion. The Chesapeake and Ohio Canal was outdistanced by the railroad before it was completed. The Erie Canal served for a period from 1829 to 1889 as a major artery of westward commerce but in time was obscured by the railroad construction along the Mohawk Corridor.

Then followed a period of canal building under government aus-

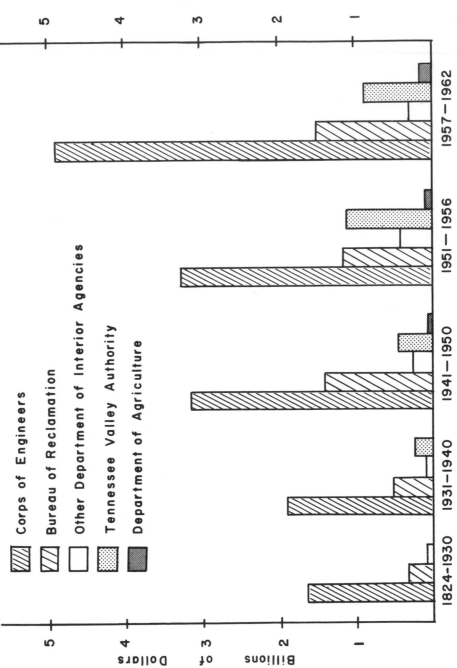

Fig. II-2—Federal Appropriations for Water Resources Development, 1824–1962. Costs are adjusted to 1958 price levels.

pices which continues up to the present day as shown in Figure II–2. From the complex history of public investment in navigation facilities, two facts should be noted. One is that the volume of investment in waterway improvement continued to be heavy, although relatively smaller by comparison with national investment in public works with each decade. The second is that over a period of 40 years a series of academic and government appraisals of waterway investment heaped increasing doubt on their economic consequences. Reports by the Brookings Institution, and a series of federal commissions, including the Second Hoover Commission, questioned whether the waterway impacts had justified their costs or fulfilled the expectations of their advocates.[14]

Resistance to Economic Challenge

Quite aside from criticism leveled at methods of computing, discounting, and comparing benefits and costs that the directives prepared by the Bureau of the Budget and published in 1962 in Senate Document 97 were intended to meet, there is doubt as to what relation waterway improvement has had to economic growth during recent decades.[15] Bulk movements of freight along the Upper Ohio, Allegheny, and Monongahela would seem without much question to warrant prior investment in the waterway, and there are a few other reaches such as the main New York channels, the Chicago Sanitary Canal, and the Mississippi below Baton Rouge which are beyond challenge. The criticism attaching to many of the other projects is that traffic has not reached expectations, that much of it is sand and gravel for channel maintenance, and that costs have grown disproportionately above estimates. By 1965 coal and petroleum products formed 60 percent of water traffic on a ton-mile basis. The average cost to shippers was about three mills per ton-mile, more than pipelines but half that for truck transport and a fifth that to rail shippers. This is not the place to weigh the bulky appraisals of the returns from waterway investment. It is appropriate, however, to inquire why the navigation program has continued over a long period in the face of heavy and sometimes bitter criticisms. Were they all ungrounded or misguided they probably would have been discredited, but their persistence suggests otherwise, and the factors at work may have a bearing on the tenacity of other types of single-purpose public construction.

Conflicts between navigation and other activities are more those of omission than commission. That is, few navigation improvements actively interfere with other water use—the Delaware and Florida canal cases are exceptions—and most waterway projects simply fail to develop opportunities which might have been garnered by a different design. Thus, there are fewer active and belligerent public groups opposed to the waterways than toward some other types of works. The groups that have suffered most have been private groups in poor repute (the railroads) rather than public groups, and few significant sets of citizen organizations have considered themselves to have been injured.

A peculiar mystique attaches to waterway improvement. It was well exemplified by Senator Kerr who to his last days felt that his great contribution to his native state would be that of bringing a deep waterway on the Arkansas River straight to the shores of Catoosa as part of a comprehensive basin plan.[16] Navigation investment is favored by a belief that new channels inevitably promote economic growth along their shores and by the fact that social costs usually fall directly on competing transport and only indirectly on citizens paying them through general taxes. This has been undergirded in a peculiar sense by the constitutional provision supporting interstate commerce, giving special credence to a federal obligation to develop the streams for that purpose alone.

Although much navigation development has been merged in multiple-purpose construction, the thread of single-purpose public and private construction is still strong. A large proportion of the new works, chiefly those small in size, are single-purpose. They are located in small tributaries or in harbors along the intra-coastal waterway and the Mississippi River system. The newer, more massive improvements are carried out for the most part as components of multiple-purpose construction projects.

In sum, the federal government carries the dominant responsibility for planning, constructing, and paying for navigation improvement. It considers a very narrow range of alternatives, restricts its research chiefly to methods of channel modification, and relies upon private shippers to innovate in technology. The economic analysis is rather rigidly formulated. The chief public constraints are in regulating the channels and common carriers. Just how much effect the improvements have had on the economy is difficult to assess. Although there has been a tendency to ignore side effects—and they have been heavy in a few canalized reaches —they have been minor in many rivers.

The Bureau of Reclamation for Arid Lands

From the Reclamation Act of 1902 until the Reclamation Project Act of 1939 the aims and methods of irrigation of dry lands under public auspices were similar in several respects to navigation. The purposes ranged from promoting national growth to resettling veterans and protecting threatened private projects. New lands were brought under cultivation and reliable supplies were provided to areas which had been over-extended.[17] Storage and river diversion programs were seen as a verdant alternative to dry land farming and grazing, with the water resource regarded as available up to the amount of the regulated mean flow as recorded. Although vigorous attention was given to engineering research on structural design, and to methods of improving water distribution and land drainage, little attention was given by the Bureau of Reclamation to innovations within the reach of individual irrigators such as sprinkler systems and pumping from deep aquifers. Yet those two advances, coupled with cheap electric power for pumps, revolutionized the practice of irrigation in both arid and humid lands during the past two decades and made it possible for individual farmers to take the initiative where water supplies permitted. Economic efficiency was measured by the government as an appraisal of indirect effects combined with ability of water users to repay under formulas in which capital was provided without interest over periods of 40–50 years. Problems of canal seepage, downstream increase in salts, channel degradation through erosion or silting, and reservoir fluctuation were distinctly secondary to the major task of irrigating new lands or preserving developed lands through public construction. Water rights were under state control and followed rather than guided new development. They were not directly manipulated by the federal agency, which made its chief contributions in providing engineering services and capital at low cost, and exercised regulation through the 160-acre limitation as an incentive to family-sized farms and through anti-speculation controls on land prices.

How much the welfare of the livestock growers or the farmers and those serving them or of the nation was advanced by these investments is, at best, speculative. While certain areas, such as Northeastern Colorado and the Yakima Valley, clearly were highly productive, others were marginal; academic debate on the returns from federal irrigation is lively, and solid studies of projects are few. As a substitute for the rugged rule of the 1890's in the Great Plains that it takes three crops of settlers to make one successful, irrigated farm, it was alleged that the government substituted the practice of paying for two crops of produce to bring one to market. Project lands suffered heavily from erosion in some areas and from salting and waterlogging in others, and the flow of mineralized water was increased through consumptive use of water and through return flows. As in the case of navigation, no attempt is made here to weigh the case because much needed evidence is lacking.

Municipal Water and Waste

Until the 1950's the record of municipal waste disposal was one of relatively little choice among a small number of treatment techniques with the predominant aims being to meet demands for dependable service and to avoid injury to human health.[18] Viewed in their hydrologic role as nature's sewers, streams and lakes were treated as depositories. Little attention was paid to alternative techniques of either reducing waste before it reaches the water body or diluting it thereafter. Economic evaluation was expressed in minimum cost terms for conventional treatment with little attempt to measure the social effects. The consequences of waste effluents on sectors other than health received secondary attention. Municipal agencies built and operated the sewers and treatment plants, and state agencies prescribed minimum standards on sanitary grounds. The tide of pollution in streams was barely stemmed. While serious threats to public health were averted, except in the epidemics of intestinal ills along the Ohio River during low-flow periods, the cost to fishlife and other stream organisms was large. Economic growth advanced at the cost of the biological ecosystems and of aesthetic enjoyment of a changing landscape.

Municipal water supply is the most dramatic example of single-purpose construction by public agencies. It will be appraised in more detail in Chapter VI in connection with its characteristic use of linear projections of demand, but it may be noted here as meeting growing urban needs without serious health hazard, as being open to techniques for treatment and more limited in views of possible supplies, and as pursuing a minimum cost approach to new investment with little regard for other areas.

The Two Strategies

Single-purpose public construction brought tremendous changes in the face of the United States. In contrast to private single-purpose construction of rural water supply, drainage, irrigation, and hydroelectric power facilities, it is remarkably free from experimentation with alternative means. It is largely impervious to doubts as to economic justification. One type of construction came to be associated with one aim by one form of public agency—municipal, district, or federal. It is a ponderous strategy using a limited number of blunt instruments, insensitive to economic indicators, and highly conservative in dealing with risk and uncertainty. Aim, method, and administrative responsibility have come to be intertwined so that the preservation of one is linked with the integrity of all: Corps of Engineers, waterway channels, and rate reductions; Bureau of Reclamation, dams, and new water or new farms; municipal sewer department, secondary treatment, and disease-free water. The strategy spells ease of execution, the creation of solid constituencies, inflexibility of method, hide-bound valuation, and a widespread deterioration in water quality in both humid and arid lands.

The single-purpose private construction strategy shows greater awareness of choices available and is more innovative in technology. Not always perceptive of differences in water availability or quality, the private manager tends to apply economic criteria carefully within certain limits, as when a homeowner selects a water supply. Its changes in the landscape tend to be more diffuse. There is little concern for the effects of the management on landscape or society, and these receive attention when uses conflict or public agencies establish regulations or competition.

Is it practicable to pursue a single public aim without accompanying rigidity? Does a shift from single aim to multiple aims change the outcome significantly? The record of the effort at flood loss reduction up through its new look in the summer of 1966 will throw light on these questions.

From Multiple Purpose to
Multiple Means: Flood Loss Reduction

III

Single-purpose construction strategies evolved in two important directions beginning in the late 1920's. Most dramatic and widespread was the shift from single-purpose to multiple-purpose public construction, as exemplified by the great systems of dams serving joint aims in the Columbia, Missouri, Ohio, and Tennessee basins. Less visible and accepted more slowly was the effort to apply different means to gaining a single goal, as revealed in the management of flood losses. Enthusiasm for the multiple-purpose strategy caught on in the mid 1930's, probably reached a zenith thirty years later, and then became the subject of somewhat jaundiced reappraisal. Application of multiple means did not receive a full national test until action on flood loss management in 1966, and its fate still hangs in the balance.

Three Concepts in Multiple-Purpose Construction

The idea of multiple-purpose water construction within entire drainage basins had its roots in technological advances of the early twentieth century which permitted low-cost construction of large dams through use of concrete and of earth moving equipment, generation of hydroelectric power, and electric energy transmission over long distances. As the technical possibilities of multiple-purpose construction were seen, three important concepts contributed to a public view of integrated river development as a prime aim of public water management.[1]

First, and probably most important, was the concept of the multiple-purpose project. Hoover Dam on the lower Colorado River is the prototype, and no structure in water management has greater significance in this respect. It was the first federal project explicitly designed to use one gigantic concrete structure to serve multiple purposes. The dam stored water to be used for irrigation of the Imperial Valley, for production of hydroelectric power, for control of floods in the lower reaches of the Colorado River, for augmenting water supply in the Southern California urban areas, and, theoretically, for enhancement of navigation on that little-traveled stream. Coming on the heels of a long period of single-purpose, single-method construction by both public and private agencies, the multiple-purpose dam was a genuine revolution in engineering techniques. It substituted one structure for a number of structures and in so doing it often gained economies of scale and of combination which otherwise would have been lost.

The second significant concept was that of planning for entire drainage basins. The drainage basin approach had its first full-fledged application in a single-purpose project for flood control in the Miami Basin by the Miami Valley Conservancy District established under authorization of the Ohio legislature following the disastrous flood of 1913. The concept was popularized through the controversy centering on solutions to the Lower Mississippi flood control problem during 1927 and was embodied in the authorization in 1928 for the Corps of Engineers to make a series of basin-wide studies of navigation, flood control, hydroelectric power, and irrigation in basins designated in House Document 308. The first of those reports provided the basis for engineering plans, albeit radically revised, by the Tennessee Valley Authority in that basin under the Tennessee Valley Act of 1933.[2] Other "308" reports gave the technical ground for major water projects, such as Fort Peck on the Missouri, which were launched under the emergency public works program which began at the same time.

TVA became the exemplar of a combination of multiple-purpose projects in an entire drainage basin with a clear intent to promote social change. On this hinged a third theme. Although some type of social change is implicit in any water management project, if only to stabilize existing agriculture or urban economy which otherwise would be threatened by flood or drought, the TVA was the first to contemplate such change throughout an entire basin and to consciously plan for shifts in income levels and modes of life. While its influence probably was greater by example outside than within the United States, even there it encountered major curbs, for while the creation of other valley authorities was widely debated, the problems of administrative application were sufficiently severe so that no country, including the United States,[3] duplicated its form of valley-wide unified management beyond an initial pilot area.

Multiple-purpose projects developed first as joint irrigation-hydroelectric power schemes under the Reclamation Act, beginning with the Salt River Project in the early 1900's, but they were not regularly embodied in basin-wide plans until Hoover Dam and the "308" reports gave more precise application to the concept. Then, with the rise of public works to cope with depression and newly recognized poverty, and against the background of the social reform that was inherent in the New Deal era, multiple-purpose basin-wide planning by public agencies gained dominance. In 1957 the importance of integrated river development was solidly supported by a United Nations panel.[4] It continued into the mid-1960's as the predominant strategy.

New Organizations

By 1940 the main characteristics of multiple-purpose public construction were clear. Although refinements were made thereafter, the essential elements remained little changed for more than two decades. In that period experimentation and much public discussion of the multiple-purpose strategy centered for the most part upon the appropriate administrative organization to prepare and carry out basin designs.[5] Experimentation with organization included a variety of federal inter-agency committees, many having their roots in the joint federal-state-local inventory of projects initiated by the National Resources (Planning) Board in 1936. With the abolition of the Board in 1943, collaboration in basin planning was continued by two successive federal inter-agency committees and through coordinating committees in major basins such as the Columbia and the Missouri. Special basin-wide studies were instituted in the Arkansas-White-Red (1950), the New England basins (1950), the Texas basins (1958), and the Southeast drainage basins (1958). Special federal-state agencies were established, beginning with the mechanism of the Upper Rio Grande Compact in 1936 and the Red River of the North investigations in 1937,[6] and most recently embodied in the Delaware River Commission of 1964.[7]

Range of Purposes

With the initiation of the Southeast Basins Study, eleven purposes commonly were contemplated in such drainage basin investigations. Specified in that authorizing act were navigation, flood control, hydroelectric power, irrigation, municipal water supply, municipal waste disposal, industrial water supply, recreation, wildlife conservation, low flow regulation, and soil conservation. The range of purposes was well established. It generally was assumed that construction programs would be prepared for entire basins or groups of basins, and that multiple-purpose projects would be designed wherever economically and politically feasible.

In most of the basin studies a similar style of analysis prevailed.[8] The procedure was to make an inventory of hydrologic and associated physical phenomena in the basin, including precipitation, runoff, groundwater, soils, agricultural land use, forest use, and related aspects of the natural environment. An economic base study was intended to build up demographic and income data as of the time of study, to assess trends in population and in production over preceding years, and to project these into the future in terms of estimated population and levels of manufacturing and agricultural activity. Upon that base, projections were made of estimated demands upon water and land for a wide variety of uses, particularly for power, irrigated land, urban water supply, and recreational facilities.

Relating Upstream to Downstream Planning

Throughout the discussions of river basin planning from the Inland Waterways Commission declarations to the Southeast Basins Study Commission findings, lip service was given to the union of upstream and downstream measures for river management.[9] In a few areas, such as in watershed protection studies of smaller tributaries of the Connecticut Basin, where the state department of agriculture employed engineering consultants to collaborate in basin planning, close integration was achieved.[10] In most areas, however, the joining of downstream engineering measures with upstream land management proved a convenience of publication rather than an actual program of complementary activity. The upstream-downstream problem illustrates acutely the difficulty of genuinely reconciling two or more purposes in a single project or basin program.

The question of whether planning for the main streams needed to go hand in hand with soil and forest management upstream was debated in theory over three decades. In 1912 the National Waterways Commission had recommended that forest and land measures did not promise sufficiently certain results to warrant modifying engineering practices downstream. Discussion of the principle of integration was heated, but glossed over several difficulties which would arise when theory would be put to practical test. This became evident in attempts under the Flood Control Act of 1936 to develop for pilot drainage areas, such as the Trinity Basin in Texas and the Little Tallahache Basin in Mississippi,[11] programs that in fact harmonized measures of land-use improvement and treatment with measures of engineering control of stream and channel in the lower reaches of the same drainage areas. From the outset, there was disagreement between the Department of Agriculture and the Corps of Engineers as to the practicability of doing so, and a tacit understanding that each agency would go its own way. But administrative troubles showed themselves promptly in contending efforts between the Forest

Service, with its woodlands interests, and the Soil Conservation Service, with its concern for cultivated lands, to carry responsibility for dealing with land-use components in upstream areas. Strains within the Department of Agriculture became acute. Review during 1940 by interested federal agencies of the Trinity River report raised agonizing doubts as to the practicability of producing integrated reports. Detailed ventures at integration were avoided, and, in time, primary responsibility for Agriculture upstream studies was given to the Soil Conservation Service.

One reason for the inability of government agencies to harmonize upstream and downstream measures was that most of the legislation and public thinking upon which it was founded assumed a precision and strength of hydrologic relationships among land-use measures and downstream flow which remained to be demonstrated. As discussed by Leopold and Maddock in *The Flood Control Controversy*,[12] some of those assumptions proved inaccurate, and others were recognized only with so many qualifications as to time and circumstance that they contributed little to the forging of genuine integrated plans. Not much could be said about downstream effects of upstream measures with sufficient confidence to justify any alteration in conventional engineering measures.

The basic difference between the Department of Agriculture and the Corps of Engineers in early flood control investigations was the difference between engineering and ecology. The engineers saw themselves as being the valiant and competent technicians who set out to curb a stream on rampage, to keep the father of waters from invading the homes of the sons of man along his shores, in short, to harness a recalcitrant nature. The Department of Agriculture people saw themselves essentially as trying to harmonize man's action with what they regarded as ecological principles so long as the measures were those which the Department customarily proposed to land owners.

Beyond the hydrologic difficulties which were momentous, as indicated in Chapter V, the difficulty of bringing together agencies with different administrative responsibilities in preparing plans for the same broad purpose by similar but not identical combination of measures proved almost insurmountable. Complications of the same order arose with respect to planning of joint irrigation, flood control, and power facilities in territories where Bureau of Reclamation and Corps of Engineers shared authority.[13]

It is noteworthy that in activities of the Department of Agriculture under the Watershed Protection Act, increasing emphasis was placed upon use of downstream engineering works. The proportion of investment in engineering works to land improvement works in projects under the Watershed Protection Act tended to increase. The Department of Agriculture sought authority to deal with larger size engineering structures, an effort meeting with resistance from the Corps of Engineers which felt that its proper territory for engineering design was being invaded as the agriculturists moved downstream.

Multiple-Purpose Decisions

Multiple-purpose construction strategy brought with it a series of changes in the nature of decisions involved. The shift from single-purpose to multiple-purpose construction had two important effects upon the *range of choice*. The first was to increase the total number of purposes perceived in public water planning by adding new purposes and by opening public and professional thinking to the possibility of including still further purposes. Although there had been no significant federal construction of reservoirs for recreation purposes, once the concept of multiple-purpose found acceptance and once Lake Mead and the early TVA reservoirs proved to have large and unsuspected value for bringing water recreation to the people of both arid and humid regions, recreation gradually gained importance in project planning under Congressional authorization. Similarly, fresh concern grew for the use of stored waters for reduction of pollution, and in most parts of the United States other than the upper Ohio Basin where the practice already was current, new projects began to include waste dilution as a possible joint purpose.

At the same time, the addition of purposes tended to sharpen recognition of the ambiguity of statements of single aims. When flood control and irrigation features were included as components in the same project it became clear that whereas flood control was to be evaluated primarily in terms of losses prevented, irrigation was to be considered more in terms of an economy to be developed than of a prevention of losses by those suffering from water shortage. To be sure, reclamation and protection were embodied in many flood-control projects, and prevention of shortage and development of new land were included in many irrigation projects, but the discrepancies became more apparent when it was necessary to house different types of analysis under the same analytical roof. Although clouded by an integrated river basin mystique, the systematic statement of aims sharpened.

The accretion of aims did not, however, affect the perception of means. The total number of means became no larger than those in use under single-purpose projects, the chief difference being that of designing multiple-purpose rather than single-purpose structures. To have considered multiple means at that stage would have opened a Pandora's box which no one felt capable of closing. There seemed to be in the middle 1930's and early 1940's a discreet kind of understanding that such possibilities would not be explored in depth. Even though the National Resources Planning Board tried strenuously to deal with the whole spectrum of technical and social actions which would shape the course of resource development, it did not find effective methods of doing so for a single basin and it avoided comparisons of resource measures with other types of measures. Study techniques were inadequate, and administrative and political pressures were inhibiting. When some members of the Department of Agriculture challenged the assumption behind the reclamation program that construction of water projects was an obviously effective means of advancing agricultural productivity in the arid regions,[14] tensions heightened so that it finally became apparent that the Department of the Interior, the Department of Agriculture, and their constituencies could best coexist by letting that issue rest undiscussed and unresolved.

Estimates of the resources of water and land involved in multiple-purpose management became progressively more refined and discerning as the years went on. One of the pervasive benefits from the shift to the multiple-purpose strategy was the inducement it offered to design and find financial means for inventory of fundamental hydrologic and land information in connection with the preparation of basin plans. The applications of precipitation, stream flow, water quality, and similar data increased. Funds from the Corps of Engineers and the Bureau of Reclamation were reallocated in modest amounts to data-collection agencies such as the U.S. Geological Survey and the Weather Bureau in order to obtain data which had not been considered essential for the more limited single-purpose undertakings. The facts of water took on greater significance as the scale of projects increased, as the number of user agencies enlarged, and as attention to the implications of data in project design became more precise.[15]

It is striking that *technology* did not change significantly during the first thirty years in which the multiple-purpose public construction strategy was in full operation. Conventional structural means were continued and while there were, to be sure, important improvements in the design of spillways, turbines, canal linings, and water treatment plants, and in the economic limits of power transmission, there were no innovations in physical methods of managing water of such a character that the form of management was altered drastically. Methods for remote recording of hydrologic data and for stream flow forecasting and routing were advanced, and waste treatment was improved.

Another important aspect of technology was that most of the structures were built upon the assumption that there would be no significant change in science or its application over the life of the projects. This ordinarily was a time horizon of 50 to 100 years. Obsolescence was not anticipated, and there was no strenuous effort to induce it through research. The irony of this aspect of strategy was that, in a period unprecedented in world history in the advance of science and its application to the everyday world of construction and consumption, the plans for using water were grounded largely on the proposition that no changes would affect either the technology of manipulating water or the demand for it. To be sure, on the basis of history, there was reason for caution. Few significant changes in water technology had occurred during the first half of the century. It was not until the 1940's that spray irrigation took on wide importance, and between the development of secondary waste treatment early in the century and the 1940's there were few major advances in sewage treatment.[16]

Economic analysis of multiple-purpose water projects underwent progressive refinement in the means of measuring flows of prospective benefits and costs, and in preparing optimal basin programs. Improvement in methodology was enhanced by the development of a new school of economic study of water resources led by the Eckstein volume in 1958 and followed shortly thereafter by the works by Krutilla and Eckstein, McKean, Tolley, and Hirshleifer, DeHaven, and Milliman. The marginal analysis was rigorous and predominantly normative; it was employed in only a few instances to judge what had happened. Solid steps were taken in determining what would be wise allocation of capital resources in the light of estimates of future economic effects. Double counting of benefits was curbed, techniques for placing quantitative values on intangible costs and benefits were devised, and the significance of opportunity cost and social rate of return was exposed.

Interest in the academic appraisal was reinforced by lively concern in economic analysis among thoughtful federal agency personnel. Here, the confrontation of different public aims in multiple-purpose feasibility studies paid large dividends in improved methods. With Bureau of the Budget leadership, guidelines for project evaluation were laid down in Circular A-47 as an outcome of the President's Water Resources Policy Commission. The "Green Book"[17] emerged as an earnest cooperative attempt to codify procedural problems faced by federal agencies. Then, in Senate Document 97 more detailed criteria were established by the Bureau of the Budget.

From both the scholarly inquiries and the administrative coping with project study emerged an effort to comprehend the economic and political implications of basin-wide planning that found enlightened guidance and expression in the Harvard Water Resources Seminar.[18] Under Maass and Hufschmidt, the Harvard group clarified thinking as to multiple-purpose planning, contributed new evaluative techniques, and gave advanced training to an influential group of federal workers. Through these and other efforts the loose kind of analysis that had flourished under the aim of preparing "basin accounts" for entire drainage areas, as reflected in the report of the President's Water Resources Policy Commission,[19] took on greater precision, and the measurement of economic consequences became more accurate.

A continuing weakness in perception of economic efficiency in multiple-purpose water management was the implicit assumption that all other aims such as income redistribution among particular regions (e.g. Appalachia) or sectors (e.g. family-size farms) were persuasive reasons for public agitation in favor of new projects. The unwillingness of the Congress to exercise more rigorous appraisal of new projects in terms of economic efficiency or the manipulation by agency personnel of study methods to get favorable benefit-cost findings sometimes are taken as violation of sound economic principles.[20] In part they may be. But they also reflect recognition of other aims. Maass' proposal to expand benefit-cost analysis to include other objectives, such as aid to Indian populations, promises to carry the evaluation of multiple-purpose construction methods to a higher and more fruitful level.[21]

With respect to *spatial linkages,* the multiple-purpose projects for the first time brought sharply into focus man's need to recognize the whole array of consequences of a single engineering work. To be sure, no project study succeeded in doing so. Indeed, the usual basin report laid heavy stress on measurable economic effects, and dealt with other effects chiefly if they promised some severe problem, as when rare wildlife habitat would be disturbed. Implications for ecosystems of water storage or of new arteries of transportation were largely ignored.

Concern for recognition of the full atmospheric, biological, geographic, and aesthetic ramifications of massive interventions in the water cycle was handicapped by lack of scientific methods to identify and measure the consequences. During the early days of federal multiple-purpose activity there was keen interest by both government agencies and citizens' groups in making arrangements so that before a new project was started all interested parties might be put on notice and given an opportunity to register complaints as to possible injuries or to suggest ways of modifying the proposal to gain supplementary returns. This was the rationale behind the attempt to coordinate new federal water construction proposals under Executive Order 9384 which had its genesis in the Presidential memorandum of 1936 requiring agencies to submit statements of impending land drainage and water storage projects for joint agency review.[22] At that stage, representatives of wildlife conservation organizations were pointing out the hazards to salmon fisheries of throwing dams across the Columbia River, and the inanity of one agency helping North Dakota farmers drain marshy lands while another assisted the neighboring farmers in restoring their drained lands to provide breeding habitat for migratory waterfowl. TVA made early provision with the Smithsonian Institution for archeological survey of prospective reservoir areas to prevent loss of evidence of prehistoric cultures, and similar studies were made in other basins as appropriate. By the mid-1950's, the Echo Park Dam project on the Green River in Utah had encountered fatal opposition because of its likely flooding of part of the Dinosaur National Monument, and in 1965 the Bridge Canyon and Marble Canyon proposals on the Colorado River in Arizona had run onto the rocks of Sierra Club opposition to flooding of parts of the Grand Canyon both in and outside of that Monument.[23]

Although these negative actions tended to focus on what appeared to be drastic threats to natural beauty and areas of special scientific interest, they symbolized a deeper kind of distress at the prospect of effecting changes in the American landscape whose significance in natural systems could not be judged accurately. This uneasiness had much in common with the advocacy of caution by Carson in *Silent Spring*.[24] It saw palpable threats to ecosystems, suspected others, and led to increasing hesitation with regard to further human interventions.

As in the history of the upstream-downstream debate, the ecological view was at a disadvantage in having little evidence to put up against the more confident engineering predictions of practical outcomes in water flow, power production, or visitor days at recreation sites. Evidence was lacking because broader investigations of the effects of water projects on stream channels, ground water, valley and upland vegetation, and fauna were not undertaken either before or after construction, and also because scientific research on ecological relations of that character commanded little widespread attention.

Social Effects

As a strategy, multiple-purpose public construction carried major benefits to the economy, but the net effects cannot be judged adequately without types of area analysis which have yet to be made. Increases in energy production, crop harvest, miles of navigable waterway, visitor days at reservoirs, or treated waste can be tallied up. The full costs and the net benefits are less easy to calculate.

Clearly, there were great economies resulting from scale and from combination in the large multiple-purpose structures. Although Krutilla has shown that the approved designs in selected areas fall short of the optimum,[25] the gains were substantial, particularly in efficient power production. Irrigation and navigation improvements were undertaken which would not have been regarded as warranted as single-purpose ventures.

A principal social loss was to be found in the influence which the large structures had upon the pace and character of social change. Based upon the assumption that existing institutional arrangements would hold for a long time period, as in the case of irrigation projects where it was believed state water law would prevail and that there would be no significant changes in the institutional means of allocating water or water shortage, the structures set the public mind in a frame which discouraged serious discussion of changing these institutions. Institution, agency, and method of construction became inseparably linked in the mind of the technician as well as with the broader public. Rather than overtly fostering social change, they tended to support the status quo.

Policies with respect to hydroelectric power and recreation stand in sharp contrast even when combined in the same project. As administered by TVA and the Department of the Interior and abetted by the Rural Electrification Administration, federal power marketing set out to reduce rates and increase consumption, favoring public and cooperative purchasers. Programs for development of recreation at federal reservoirs tended to conform to whatever was the prevailing policy of the state with respect to fees and discrimination among users.[26]

The shift from single-purpose to multiple-purpose construction had the early effect of reducing the direct participation of private managers in most aspects of water management involved in the new projects. Irrigators and irrigation districts contracted for new works through the federal bureau. Local levee and drainage districts in the alluvial valley of the Mississippi were restricted to influencing and making contributions of land and rights of way to the comprehensive project, under the Mississippi River Commission; and in other areas where state districts had been organized, as in the Muskingum Conservancy District of Ohio, responsibility for major decisions shifted toward the Corps of Engineers.[27] Inclusion of domestic water supply, waste dilution, and recreation facilities in the large new reservoirs increased federal participation in those activities. It also had the countervailing effect of requiring more vigorous organization of state agencies which were called upon to contribute technical review of plans, financial support, and management of facilities.

All along, the role of state agencies was in flux. In the 1930's the only state which had both ambition and competence to draw up multiple-purpose plans was California with its program for the Central Valley, a vision which stimulated federal planning for the same area and twenty years later led to the State Water Plan. When the National Resources Board in 1936 made the first national attempt to consult with state and local groups on programs of public works for all of the country's river basins, many states were hard put to find means of assembling technical opinions and relevant information. The organization of state planning agencies was one measure taken by the Board to help fill this gap as part of a larger effort at comprehensive area planning. Some of the state boards flourished for a time; most gradually transformed their activities so as to have less direct involvement in water planning. In their places the states were represented increasingly by state water engineers, water conservation boards, departments of water and forests, and similar agencies which were obliged to enter into contracts for participation in paying local contributions to federal flood or water supply facilities or in managing reservoir recreation areas. Their competence was called into question especially when, under procedures established by the Congress in the Coordination Act of 1944, each state was invited to submit comments on proposed reports by federal agencies. Often, a state office with a handful of professional workers was expected in a few months to make critical comments and suggestions on a detailed plan involving scores of projects that had been prepared by a well-staffed federal agency over a period of five years. The response was necessarily superficial, sometimes fragmented, and frequently directed at either basic issues of policy or at a currently troublesome dispute over a particular design. One promising feature of the Water Resources Planning Act of 1965 was its provision of support to state agencies, subject to matching contributions, to assist them in more precise and hopefully imaginative planning in which multiple purposes received balanced attention.

Environmental Effects

Three statements can be ventured about the effects of multiple-purpose projects on the environment. The consequences undoubtedly were widespread. They were extremely difficult to trace out in their effects upon atmosphere, water regimen, and ecosystems. On balance, gains probably outweighed losses in most areas, but firm conclusions cannot be drawn.

Construction of the new dams, channels, and canals brought gigantic changes in the volume of stored water, the habitat and bed of stream reaches, and the area of irrigated and drained land. As already indicated, many of the relationships to systems of air, water, silt, and living communities have not been pursued sufficiently to support refined judgments as to the long-term results. For example, the influence of storage on the sediment accumulations and channel capacity of downstream reaches has been investigated only in a few streams. Certain of the effects, such as those on malaria vectors, were well enough understood so that injurious impacts could be prevented. In other cases, such as shifts in aquatic life induced by storage, observations of change have been made and fishing improvements have been designed.[28]

It seems likely but not certain that most of the deleterious short-term consequences over a few decades have been identified in some fashion, that the long-term consequences remain to be measured, and that in the greater number of instances the damages do not yet appear so serious as to outweigh the benefits which have accrued to society.

Concept of Multiple Means

The most recent and incisive statement of the deficiencies of a single-means approach where multiple purposes are involved is in the recent report by the Committee on Water of the National Academy of Sciences —National Research Council entitled *Alternatives in Water Management*.[29] Senate Document No. 97 had directed that:

> Planning for the use and development of water and related resources shall be on a fully comprehensive basis so as to consider ...
> (2) All relevant means (including nonstructural as well as structural measures) singly, in combination, or in alternative combinations reflecting different basic choice patterns for providing such uses and purposes. (p. 3)

The report to the Secretary of the Army by the Civil Works Study Board had extended this view by saying:

> ... the Chief of Engineers should—
> (f) Improve plan formulation through increased consideration and presentation of alternatives in reports. (p. 19)

The Corps began to take steps to put this view into action.

As presented in the *Alternatives* report, the concept is summed up as follows:

> A review of current efforts to manage water to serve the needs and desires of man reveals that all aspects of water management

would be improved by planning that would maintain flexibility for the future, foreclose as few choices as practicable, and put fresh demands on science to predict consequences and to provide alternatives to meet changing needs. Specifically, such an emphasis would call for applying more intensively present knowledge of the behavior of water, land, and man in two ways: first, by identifying all available alternatives for coping with water problems and taking systematic steps to discover new alternatives; and second, by improving methods of recognizing the social as well as the physical consequences of water management and of weighing alternatives. (p. 48)

When efforts to reduce flood losses and to curb water pollution are cited, alternatives are viewed as embracing alternatives in goal, engineering measures, other management measures, institutional arrangements, timing and size, and location. The idea that the same goal may be sought through a variety of engineering and management means is basic but not widely practiced.

Evolving Policy for Managing Flood Losses

The Committee on Water's reference to flood loss reduction as an example of an opportunity to replace single-means management may be expanded with profit because there is a clear-cut history of the evolution of the idea of multiple means in dealing with flood losses, and because federal management policy recently has shifted in that direction. The earliest flood control was ostensibly a single-purpose enterprise but it involved a continuing fugue of interweaving themes of protection and reclamation by engineering means, and it included alternative measures such as flood warnings and relief.

The administrative policy of dealing with flood loss reduction chiefly by single means changed when President Johnson sent a message and accompanying report and executive order to the Congress in August, 1966.[30] The federal flood control program had been like a heroic effort to curb fires by putting them out with modern equipment while paying little attention to what causes the fires. Engineering measures to curb floods were effective in many places, yet the national toll of flood losses continued to mount as more hazard areas were occupied and little attention was paid to the extent to which increases in flood damage might be warranted by the returns to the nation.[31] Under the new policy, the Corps of Engineers was to continue to build flood protection projects where economically feasible, but it was to work with other federal, state, and local agencies in encouraging wiser use of flood plains. Provision was made that new federal installations, highway locations, urban renewal schemes, and mortgage insurance be undertaken only after careful weighing of the flood hazard. Recognizing that many of the crucial decisions about flood plain development are made by the private property owner, government agencies now would join in giving him information about flood hazard and ways of coping with it in circumstances that would permit him to choose alternatives in awareness of the consequences.

Against the background of federal involvement in coping with flood losses it may be asked why the view of exploring management alternatives has taken so long to gain acceptance. In other types of water management as well, the tendency has been to narrow rather than broaden the range of choice. To what extent is this an inevitable part of the adoption of new techniques for managing a natural resource?

The Inland Waterways Commission report was among the first to state specifically that while engineering measures may be necessary to reduce flood losses by channeling streams, by embanking them with levees, or by holding water in storage or detention reservoirs, there were other means open to man.[32] These included his planning the use of the flood plains so as to minimize losses and, more important in the eyes of the Commission, the management of land upstream so as to reduce the magnitude and frequency of flood flows. When the first major federal commitment to flood control occurred with the undertaking of a co-ordinated system of levees in the alluvial valley of the lower Mississippi in 1917, all emphasis was on engineering works to reduce flood crests.

The levees-only approach was challenged after the flood disaster of 1927 when it became apparent that the old combination of channel improvement and levees would not alone prevent the giant Mississippi from occasionally breaking out of its banks and inundating sectors of the alluvial valley. The controversy which grew following the 1927 flood as to suitable remedial measures was of two sorts. One had to do with whether it was desirable to undertake further engineering works on the lower river in contrast to carrying out land use measures in the tributaries. This centered on the assertions by foresters that the long-term solution rested in land use management which would cause the reduction of flood flows.[33] The second was whether levees combined with channel improvements would be adequate to curb flows downstream. Here, the possibility of engineering construction of floodways was seriously explored and became an essential feature of the revised engineering plan. The possibility of building upstream storage reservoirs was explored and eliminated as being unduly expensive and uncertain.

The comprehensive project for the lower Mississippi as authorized in the Flood Control Act of 1928 was limited to engineering works in the alluvial valley but held out the possibility of exploring upstream measures in the form of reservoirs. Emphasis was on investigating other purposes of water control rather than on alternative means of reducing flood losses.

By 1936 when the floods of the Ohio and Northeastern states again placed flood control on the national agenda, the "308" reports had become more widely available and the controversy of upstream versus downstream use broke into the open in the drafting of an act to establish federal responsibility for flood control on a national scale. The Flood Control Act of that year authorized the Corps of Engineers to move ahead with study and construction of engineering works, and enabled the Department of Agriculture to carry out studies of upstream land alternatives. Both sets of measures were intended to reduce flood losses by modifying flood flows. Other types of measures to manage losses were not specified. Nor was the public mind friendly to the exploration of alternatives.[34] Editorial suggestions that other measures such as flood-proofing or land use regulation might be in order were met with coolness or hostility, and the Agriculture-Engineers debate put no weight on them.[35]

Six years later it was suggested that an integrated federal policy for dealing with flood losses would involve an examination of methods of controlling floods, insuring against damages, regulating flood plain use, and advising occupants of ways of minimizing flood losses through structural and emergency adjustments.[36] Hoyt and Langbein in their classic work on floods pursued the same theme more eloquently but without major effect upon the survey methods of the federal and state agencies proposing new flood control expenditures.[37] Evidence accumulated that the federal programs were effective in curbing flows along many stream reaches but not in curbing the national bill for losses. The Tennessee Valley Authority, after sobering experience with investment in flood control works without substantial reduction in total flood hazard in the area, began to look into alternative means, chiefly in terms of land use regulation. It became the first construction agency to pay systematic attention to the possibilities that losses could be reduced by other means than by levees, channels, and reservoirs.[38] Engineering measures generally were still viewed as more dependable than social measures. By the time of the Senate Select Committee on National Water Resources in 1961, this view was more widely embraced and was supported by the highly influential report by the Tennessee Valley

Authority on its own experience in canvassing alternative measures.[39]

The results of research on changes in use of the nation's flood plains were part of the evidence at a national conference on flood plain problems in Chicago in 1958,[40] and the recommendations of that group contributed to the establishment of a program of flood plain information studies under the Corps.

An important turning point came in 1965 when the Director of Civil Works for the Corps of Engineers, General Graham, addressing the powerful Rivers and Harbors Congress, said:

> No matter how you look at it, in our increasingly crowded land each flood-vulnerable valley needs a well-planned cooperative program of flood-plain land-use regulation combined with a progressive system of flood protection works.

Budget Task Force

By 1965 the Bureau of the Budget, reviewing projects which were proposed for authorization in the new civil works authorization bill, encountered a series of questions which led it to doubt the wisdom of continuing with the present policy. The chief points that were raised in a memorandum which put together thinking generated by discussion with the Corps of Engineers and other federal agencies at that time included the effectiveness of flood plain information reporting, means of setting desirable degrees of protection, the trend toward justifying protection projects on the basis of projected encroachment, and the effect of cost-sharing policy. Of these, the most dramatic argument was that relating to land development, where it was recognized that in some projects more than 50 percent of the expected project benefits were to result from the reclamation of new land rather than from the protection of land that already was in use for either agricultural or urban purposes.

This led to the appointment of a special task force in early autumn of 1965. The task force came at a time when there was a peculiar and fortuitous conjunction of forces. The rising proportion of expected project benefits devoted to reclamation of new lands had become abundantly evident in projects where large sums were to be spent for control of floods in areas not then occupied, but which might be developed once protection had been provided.[41] The Tennessee Valley Authority activities increasingly showed the practicability of joining engineering and hydrologic studies with urban studies in conjunction with state and local planning officials.

A new series of citizen groups concerned with other possible uses of flood plains had found expression in federal programs. Federal involvement in urban highway planning had expanded. The wildlife groups under the Land and Water Conservation Act were giving vigorous consideration to acquisition of wet lands for the preservation of nesting and breeding places for migratory waterfowl. Under the Outdoor Recreation Act of 1964, federal and state agencies for the first time were embarked on a program of acquiring or developing land in circumstances which made it possible for local interest groups to espouse schemes to preserve stream banks or wet lands for recreation purposes with federal support. The Department of Housing and Urban Development was finding it possible to combine redevelopment schemes with reduction in flood losses, and was concerned with curbing the construction in hazard areas of houses with guaranteed mortgages.

Finally, the repetition of flood disasters in the Northeastern states had stirred talk, in the Office for Emergency Planning and related civil defense agencies, of the possibility of a blanket single-premium kind of insurance coverage against all natural disasters.

The task force consulted fully with the interested federal agencies and Congressional committee staff while the report was being drafted, and the Bureau of the Budget circulated a draft among the agencies for comment before government action or public release. By the time the report was formally adopted many of its recommendations already had been accepted by the agencies and had been made a part of their operating procedure. The aim was not to get a report which would make headlines but to prepare a report in such a way that its major aims would be achieved within the limits of Congressional policy before reaching the public.

A Federal Flood Loss Reduction Program

The major results as endorsed by the principal interested agencies and approved by the President may be summarized as follows:

To improve basic knowledge about flood hazard
1. a. The immediate listing of all urban areas with flood problems so as to alert the responsible agencies.
   b. Preparation of maps and aerial photographs by the U.S. Geological Survey of reconnaissance delimitation of hazard areas.
   c. Stepping up of the Corps of Engineers and Tennessee Valley Authority flood plain information reports.
2. Action to reach agreement by federal agencies on a set of techniques to be used in determining flood frequencies.
3. A national program by the Corps of Engineers and Department of Agriculture for collecting more useful data on flood

damages, using decennial appraisals, continuing records on sample reaches, and making special surveys after unusual floods.

4. Research to gain greater knowledge as to:
    a. Problems of flood plain occupance, by Departments of Housing and Urban Development and Agriculture.
    b. Urban hydrology under the U.S. Geological Survey and HUD.

To coordinate and plan new developments on the flood plain

5. Specification by the Water Resources Council of criteria for regulation of flood plains and for treatment of flood plain problems.

6. Steps to assure that state and local planning would take proper and consistent account of flood hazard in:
    Federal mortgage insurance (Federal Housing Administration and Veterans Administration)
    Comprehensive local planning (HUD)
    Urban transport planning (Bureau of Public Roads)
    Recreational open space and development planning (Bureau of Outdoor Recreation)
    Urban open space acquisition (HUD)
    Urban renewal (Urban Renewal Administration and Corps of Engineers)
    Sewer and water facilities (HUD, Agriculture, Department of Health, Education and Welfare, and Economic Development Administration.)

7. Encouragement by the Office of Emergency Planning, Small Business Administration, and Treasury Department of consideration of relocation and floodproofing in rebuilding in flooded areas.

8. A directive to all federal agencies to consider flood hazard in locating new facilities.

To provide technical services to managers of flood plain property

9. Collection and dissemination of information by the Corps of Engineers, in collaboration with The Department of Agriculture and HUD, on alternative methods of reducing flood losses.

10. An improved system of flood forecasting under the Environmental Science Services Administration.

To move toward a practical national program for flood insurance

11. A study by HUD of the feasibility of insurance. (This had been launched and was carried out in a greatly abbreviated form

under the authority of the Southeast Hurricane Disaster Relief Act of 1965.)

To adjust federal flood control policy to sound criteria for changing needs

12. Broadened survey authorizations for the Corps of Engineers and Agriculture.
13. Provision by the Congress for more suitable cost sharing by state and local groups.
14. Reporting of flood control benefits so as to distinguish protection of existing improvements from development of new property.
15. Authorization by the Congress to include land acquisition as part of flood control plans.
16. Authorization by the Congress of broadened authority to make loans to local interests for their contributions.

It would be sanguine to suggest that all of these results will come quickly or necessarily firmly. Caution would be in order if for no other reason than the number and diversity of agencies responsible for carrying out the recommendations.[42] However, a public commitment has been made to pursue them and a new direction has been set.

Factors Affecting Adoption of Multiple Means

In seeking to explain why it took so long for this view to be adopted, reasons may be found for thinking it will take still longer for the view, once adopted, to be put into operating practice in the river valleys of the United States. Six main factors seem to have been at work. First, the controversy between the Department of Agriculture and the Corps of Engineers over upstream versus downstream measures was so bitter and protracted that it obscured discussion of other and more important alternatives to the engineering measures. The two agencies had little incentive to investigate measures that might offset their more conventional programs.

Second, it clearly was easier to manipulate a single engineering tool than several more intricate tools, such as insurance or land use regulation, to achieve the same end. Wherever presented with the opportunity to use one tool to the exclusion of several, a public agency tends to choose the simpler device. Faced with the difficulty of choosing among several measures and of seeking legislative support for them, it avoids complicating the picture.

Third, there was heavy support from contractors as well as local engineers for pursuing tried construction measures.

Fourth, most of the new federal policy with respect to floods comes in the trail of crises precipitated by flood disasters. Crises seem peculiarly unsuited to promoting consideration of complex and less well understood alternatives in contrast to simple, dramatic, and highly visible panaceas, and thus the bias toward the latter measures remains strong.

Fifth, the application of alternatives such as floodproofing, insurance, and land use regulation requires refinements of techniques and administrative devices for which there was little precedent. To these only a bit of research had been devoted and the emphasis upon normative economic analysis of tried alternatives did not stimulate their exploration.

Finally, and probably most important, so long as no one agency was charged with the responsibility for dealing with flood loss reduction rather than for carrying out a particular measure, the alternatives received little attention. For example, when local groups first challenged the applicability of zoning authority to flood loss reduction no agency addressed itself promptly to getting to the bottom of questions of legal authority and planning experience. TVA was the first to do so.

Other factors no doubt were at work, but these appear to have been most significant. Flood control serves as a striking example of the way in which commitment to largely single means obscured consideration of multiple means over the years in which the multiple-purpose dam flourished.

The same inquiry as to why alternative means were not considered could be raised for others among the multiple purposes. It was common for the Corps of Engineers to design navigation channels with little examination of alternative measures, such as carrier design, for improving transport facilities. In the case of water supply, the characteristic response to urban growth was to seek more water rather than to reduce use or provide reuse. New irrigation projects were designed to provide more food from irrigation, among other purposes, with no systematic consideration of alternative means of enhancing food supply such as supplemental irrigation in humid areas, drainage, and improved seeds. Waste disposal followed the approach of examining ways of diluting the waste in a natural stream with relatively little attention to ways of reducing the waste itself before it reached the stream, or to means of improving stream quality other than by dilution. Private power producers found it easier to turn from hydro to thermal sources. Individual farmers were rather flexible in adopting or abandoning irrigation as one method of increasing crop yields.

In coping with flood losses, private managers seemed more disposed to explore the whole range of possible means than public managers:

with ingenuity, they devised flood-forecasting and warning systems, per-suaded insurance companies to write special risk policies, and invented ways of keeping water out of their buildings. But they did this without government assistance and in the face of public policy that encouraged them to think that the viable choices were between bearing the losses or seeking a federal protection project.

Likewise, the private single-purpose managers of irrigation, domes-tic water supply, and hydroelectric programs were in many instances quicker to adopt alternative means than their public peers.

Multiple-Means Decisions

While it is too early to judge how this multiple-means strategy affects the character of flood plain management decisions and their social and environmental impacts, a few of the likely results may be predicted. The door now is open for each federal agency to take account of what it considers the full range of choice in dealing with flood loss reduction even if it is not authorized to carry out the more promising measures. For the first time, the private manager will be given technical help in recognizing the choices open to him.

Publication of the reconnaissance and flood plain information studies will make it possible for both private and public managers to estimate the flood hazard more accurately, and a series of administra-tive arrangements will require conscious assessment of the hazard as well as of potentialities for land use. Public initiative will be taken to develop new techniques, such as floodproofing and insurance, to cope with flood losses, and to disseminate knowledge of all available tech-niques.

The form of economic analysis will not be changed but it will be stimulated in more instances, and assessment of relative costs and bene-fits of different adjustments will be promoted. Insofar as insurance pre-miums are set in proportion to risk, they will provide a handy and ex-plicit measure of cost against which prospective private or public returns from flood plain use can be gauged. Just how effective will be the pre-scribed efforts to anticipate the impacts of such uses on other activities it is difficult to estimate; much will depend upon the depth of research on land uses and their consequences. To achieve these changes in the decision process will call for clarity of vision as to the aims of water management, intensity of scientific research on alternatives, and a style of administrative cooperation which thus far has been lacking.

This array of experience suggests that a strategy of multiple means may be more likely to evolve from a strategy of multiple-purpose con-

struction or single-purpose private construction than from single-purpose public construction. Once committed to a single set of means, a
public agency finds it difficult to explore the other sets of opportunities,
as illustrated by the reluctance of the Bureau of Reclamation to investigate new forms of sprinkler irrigation in the arid states or to study
supplemental irrigation or wet land reclamation in the humid East—
a reluctance enforced by Department of Agriculture opposition to any
extension of the Bureau's jurisdictional boundaries with respect to land
management in the 17 Western states. Vigorous experimentation with
individual sprinkler irrigation came primarily in the private sector.
Incisive comparison of the merits of thermal power with both hydro
power and nuclear fuel came chiefly from private power companies;
the TVA was a pioneer in comparing thermal and hydro power, while
as late as 1966 the Bureau in the Colorado Basin was arguing that it
lacked authority to make such comparisons.

There also is reason to think that research on the effects of water
management may promote consideration of alternatives whereas refinement of normative methods of evaluating projects initially may foreclose alternatives by directing attention to conventional solutions for
which acceptable computations are more readily made. When evaluative methods are turned to other alternatives, as was the case in the mid
1960's with studies of the relative economic effects of flood protection,
floodproofing, emergency measures, land acquisition, and land use regulation in flood plains,[43] new horizons are defined for the operating agencies. But even in the case of flood loss management no significant public
investment was made in research on practicable technical alternatives
such as floodproofing and land use regulation. Flood forecasting received only modest attention, and warning systems to apply the fore-
casts were largely neglected until 1966.

In considering whether or not it may be practicable to combine
the mutiple-purpose and multiple-means strategies in a single strategy,
at least three broad problems arise. One is the question of how aims
reflecting human preferences may be recognized and stated more accurately. A second is the extent to which scientific research can be expected to play a role in managing both preferences and methods. The
third is whether or not there is any practicable framework in which a
program taking careful account of changing aims and multiple means
can be pursued. These are the topics of the following chapters.

Resolving Ambiguity: What the Public Wants in Water Quality

IV

The Congress of the United States, like the people it represents, rarely has retreated from decision because its aims were confused. Most public construction for water management harbors ambiguity of expected outcomes under labels of conventional single and multiple purposes. No sector of national water management reveals this in larger degree than efforts at enhancing and protecting the quality of streams and lakes. And no sector presents more sharply the twin problems of (1) how ambiguity can be resolved if, indeed, it should be, and (2) how judgments can be made of public preferences for that quality of environment in which people seek to live their lives and which they covet for their children.

Why Manage Water?

Where private single-purpose construction is practiced, the aims generally are clear even though secondary aims are included. Farmers seeking water for domestic use may also want to care for livestock needs. Supply for fire fighting may or may not be prescribed as a purpose. Whatever they may be, the aims can be identified with little ambivalence. Private power companies for all of their expressed concern for building the regional economy do so by generating hydroelectric power in a way that will maximize net returns or assure continued dominance of a market. Although the price schedules of municipal water suppliers in some instances are designed to bolster the local government income, the private companies have held rather closely to the aim of survival, recognizing that the long-term demand for their product as well as the security of their franchise will be affected by the quality and foresight of their service.

Public construction of what has been termed single-purpose programs usually combined several aims rather loosely. The aims of promoting efficient national growth have run alongside of efforts to favor particular regions or social groups and to regulate sectors of the economy.[1] At times, harnessing an unexploited resource has been viewed as a good in itself. The federal flood control effort, it has been shown, sought to combine the prevention of damages to existing property with the protection of land which might then be used more productively. The two aims appear in differing proportions along a continuum from an established Ohio River town having no vacant land and little prospect for growth to a California town where protection will trigger intensive new development on vacant flood plains. From its onset the reclamation program sought to provide irrigation as a means of fostering growth in the arid and semi-arid states, of promoting the prosperity of family-sized farms, and of stabilizing the existing irrigated and livestock agriculture which suffered from occasional water or forage shortage. Finding homes for returning veterans figured for a time. In public hydroelectric projects, regional development was mixed with efforts to regulate rates of private producers. Navigation projects were advanced both to stimulate economic growth and to gain reductions in rail freight rates. A contributing factor in most of the agitation for all types of public construction is the belief that expenditure of construction funds in itself invigorates the communities concerned. Linked with this is the conviction that landing a project for the local district enhances both its prestige and the likelihood that the responsible legislator will be reelected. Many an American community has been uncertain as to whether it wanted a navigation channel to stimulate river traffic, and thereby industry, to lower rail rates for existing shippers, to raise the inflow of cash while the project is under construction, to improve its local image, or some combination of these.

All of these aims were merged in the multiple-purpose projects in the period of the mid 1930's when an additional aim of economic stabilization through employment-creating construction was dominant, and gave the grounds for launching large projects such as Grand Coulee and Fort Peck which otherwise would have been slow in beginning because of doubts as to their economic justification.

With new public initiative and enlarged multiple purposes, the difficulty of defining aims was magnified. In trying to serve a series of aims in one basin plan the engineer attempted to harmonize a variety of purposes that were not reconciled in the basic legislation. In doing so he used analytical methods that did not permit rigorous comparison of either the aims or the techniques applied. The federal program to curb water pollution presents under one administrative roof the complications of defining and reconciling a set of loosely stated purposes. Not all aims of pollution abatement can be served simultaneously without valuing some more highly than others and without confronting differences in human preferences.

What Is Clean Water?

The current search for water quality standards displays the difficulties dramatically. What is clean water? Could it be water whose physical, chemical, and bacteriological condition is unaffected in any way by the works of man? Water in its natural state varies tremendously from place to place, and man sometimes makes it more useful by his works. The answer is no easier if the question is put negatively. What is polluted water? A standard of cleanliness—or pollution—implies a human judgment as to suitability for particular human use at a particular time and place. Here is a basic problem of water management. Any effort to maintain or enhance the quality of water requires a definition of the uses to which it may be put and a judgment of the human preferences for each of those uses in a specific setting of water and land. It occurs at the sweeping level of national policy and at the restricted level of a short reach of stream.

Under the Water Quality Act of 1965, the states are given an opportunity to formulate what the Secretary of the Interior would establish as water quality standards "to protect the public health or welfare, enhance the quality of water and serve the purposes of this Act. In establishing such standards . . . shall take into consideration their use and value for public water supplies, propagation of fish and wildlife, recreational purposes, agricultural, industrial, and other legitimate uses." Latitude is allowed to do so upon a regional basis. Local groups have large opportunity to advance those purposes they favor. The standards are to comprise criteria of water quality and plans for enforcing them. Criteria can apply to either effluents or to streams. Inevitably they set some limit on the character of waste discharged into streams from municipalities, industries, and farms, and they involve cost to those who dispose of waste or to those who are obliged to use waters requiring further treatment. The Act does not specify criteria and methods of enforcement, and it does not indicate what preference is to be given one use over another. In the guidelines issued by the Secretary of the Interior in 1966, it is suggested that no standard should be approved which would provide for "less than existing" quality or for the sole or principal use of any stream for transporting waste, but this does not set a precise criterion of quality and it does not come to grips with the question of which users would be expected to share in the cost of treating either waste or water.[2]

In a strict sense every stream is naturally polluted for some natural use: differences in turbidity, alkalinity, dissolved oxygen, and temperature, as well as in trace elements, place severe limits upon the biota which can survive. When human uses are considered it is plain that the criteria for one use may not be consistent with those for another: fish life requires various minimum amounts of dissolved oxygen while industrial users know that the smaller the amount of dissolved oxygen the smaller their costs from corrosion of equipment; a completely clear, distilled water which would be ideal for indoor swimming would not support desirable stream fauna. The question of what is clean water can be resolved for any one water body only in terms of preferences among uses and by users as interpreted by agencies responsible for stream flow and quality. There nevertheless has been a widespread effort to set up standards of cleanliness which would apply uniformly to stream reaches, states, or the nation as a whole.

Ambiguity Has Its Charms

Ambiguity should not be condemned out of hand. In dealing with water quality standards, as in some other fields of resource management, it has several attractive attributes. It permits a high degree of administrative discretion in carrying out a program, as displayed most notably in the land planning field where under the Multiple-Purpose Use Act of 1960, the Forest Service, lacking precise definition by the Congress as to how the uses are to be reconciled, is free to exercise its own judgment. Such ambiguity also allows for large flexibility in standards from time to time and place to place as needs, perception, and technology change. It may prevent floors from becoming ceilings in enforcement proceedings. It often averts head-on confrontations until such time as a mediating path can be found, as in the case of the long delay in clarifying divergent policies of federal agencies in developing recreational facilities on reservoir margins. This may be preferred to a specific statement of aim, such as incorporated in the Transportation Act of 1966 for judging the feasibility of new navigation projects, which, once enacted, curbs any direct effort to make them comparable to other transportation improvements. Indeed, ambiguity may invite creative search for new formulations that otherwise would be inhibited by pat, readily interpreted directives.[3] The task of placing pervasive, inchoate human yearnings for space and variety and a sense of natural harmony into neat compartments is at best baffling. It is worth pursuing with imagination and without the fetters of a detailed set of instructions.

Wolman makes a strong case for administrative flexibility in setting standards of stream cleanliness, noting that virtually all the wide variations among states in permissible limits are "relatively unsupported by anything but precedent, imagination, ingenuity, enthusiasm, and nostalgia," and that:

> Almost every situation on almost every body of water in this coun-
> try is a problem in itself. As a rule, the solution to such problems is
> not assisted materially by referring to a convenient handbook. The
> solution lies in most instances in the considered balancing of tech-
> nical and financial conveniences and equities, out of which the
> perennial compromises of judgments ensue. In more instances than
> one, any criterion, in law or in rule, which stands in the way of
> these compromises is unfortunate. They lead either to unwise and
> unwarranted expenditures or to acrimonious debate and delay in
> correctives. Administrative judgment and decision are the results
> of intelligent diagnostic techniques, bargaining, availability of the
> dollar, and adaptability to the local scene. They are not and never
> have been the result of legislative fiat, even when this is re-inforced
> by formulas of pseudo-mathematical character.[4]

For some technicians and administrators the handbook rule or legislative fiat are convenient crutches. They minimize thinking, simplify
the assessment of values, and avoid the personal stress of judging degrees
of public risk.

Thus, there is a part of man which resists confusion and tries to give
convenient order to it. He persists in seeking to resolve ambiguity. He
may end in frustrated defeat, as when he declines to define a national
reclamation program so that it has the same meaning to all sectors of
the nation. He may settle into a comfortable decision to live with mod-
erate disorder and make the best of it, as when he adopts different criteria for judging competing types of transportation improvements. He
may use the search as a base for more imaginative exploration, as when
he persists in trying to set standards of water quality and devises new
instruments to state them. Any faculty member who has shared in a
curriculum committee attempt to define educational aims and programs
will have experienced all three of these reactions. It is in anticipation
of the more imaginative exploration that the question can be pursued
further, in asking how the public goes about finding out its preferences.

Types of Water Quality Standards

The need for curbing deterioration in water quality was voiced by the
Inland Waterways Commission in 1908:

> The increasing pollution of streams by soil wash and other
> waste substances connected with a growing population reduces the
> value of the water for manufacturing purposes, and renders the

water supply for communities injurious to and often destructive of human life. The prevention of these evils should be considered in any scheme of inland waterway improvement. (p. 20)

A year later a rough definition of water quality came in a report of the National Conservation Commission, a report which found little public acceptance or official recognition, and concentrated upon navigation opportunities.

> Refuse from household, farm, factory, mine, and city should be prevented from polluting streams, or extending needlessly into ground water or contaminating the air. In rural households and communities refuse should be treated as to yield high-grade fertilizer; urban sewage should be converted and utilized as a source of municipal revenue; and mine refuse should be treated as a by-product. (p. 46)

The statement does reflect a largely inchoate urge to protect the cleanliness of water courses and aquifers. Consider the difficulties which the body politic would have in 1909 or 1966 in deciding the extent to which any refuse should be prevented from polluting a stream and above what limits water pollution is believed to occur. Part of the ambiguity arises from the diverse group of people who use water. The interests include industrialists who regard water as an instrument of production, city dwellers who value water for recreation purposes or for domestic supply, wildlife managers and recreationists who look upon water as having aesthetic values or as being a medium for cultivating fish and waterfowl, farmers who draw on water for irrigation or livestock, and shippers who use streams for transport.

Within each sector of concerned citizenry there also is doubt as to the quality which should be sought for that particular group. This is as true of industrialists as it is of fish managers. While there are some rather simple standards that can be established such as the relation between concentration of mineral salts and the accumulation of scale in boilers or as to the relation between boron content and the growth of plants irrigated by that water, most of the so-called standards or criteria are relatively rough rule of thumb characteristics which are presumed to have relation to characteristics of life which people value.

Even the first and now standard measure of suitability of water for human use in terms of bacteriological content—the count of coliform organisms—is controversial. It is a simple measurement of the concentration of coliform bacteria, an organism commonly associated with excreta from human and animal intestines in temperate climates. In the 1890's a method of measuring the total number of such bacteria was developed, and was refined over the next 25 years. Today it is used around the world as a measure of water pollution but without detailed knowledge of the extent to which coliform density is directly related to disease. The count itself can vary drastically over short reaches of a stream. The recommended maximum permissible count of coliform organisms per 100 ml. has ranged from 50 to 2,400. From one standpoint, this rough assessment may be enough: the sanitary engineer can play safe by saying that so long as not more than 10 percent of the samples show positive coliforms there is little threat to health. From another standpoint, it may be said that evidence is lacking that significant viruses may not be related to coliforms, that a smaller concentration might not be associated with dangerous disease in some situations, or that a much larger concentration of organisms of animal origin might not be entirely tolerable in others.

Moreover, the perfection of chlorination and other treatment as killers of bacteria made it possible for public water suppliers to eliminate health threats from that direction (loads up to 10,000 coliform per 100 ml. could be handled) and encouraged them to carry out a low level of chlorination for generally coliform-free supplies as a safety precaution, albeit with occasional offenses to taste and odor. With such capacity to curb disease, how free should the natural source be of coliform organisms?

Similar questions can be raised about most of the other measures of water quality. For example, the measure of minimal 4 milligrams of dissolved oxygen per liter which was used by the Wollman group in its reports for the Senate Select Committee on National Water Resources, except in regions of "water shortage," was taken from very limited experiments.[5] The figures have not been established as being of critical value in other streams. Nevertheless, they are used widely and in the recent case of engineering planning for the Potomac a similar measure was taken, after a search for more precise criteria among sanitary engineers, as the gospel word for the design of huge upstream water storage and regulation works.[6]

A typical analysis of quality of water for municipal purposes today includes measures of coliform organisms, turbidity, color, odor, and concentrations of arsenic, fluoride, lead, selenium, silver, barium, cadmium, chromium, and cyanide. For both health and industrial purposes it might also include measures of alkyl benzene sulfonate, alkalinity, calcium, chloride, dissolved solids, hardness, iron, magnesium, manganese, nitrate, phosphate, potassium, radioactivity, silica, sodium, specific conductance, and sulfate.[7] An examination of water for irrigation purposes might gauge salt concentration, sodium absorption ratio, and such toxic ions as boron, sodium and chloride. Determinations of water quality for aquatic life would include acidity, ammonia, carbon dioxide, conductivity, hardness, dissolved oxygen, temperature, toxicants, and turbidity.[8]

When the first drinking water standards were drawn up by the U.S. Public Health Service in 1914 governing quality of water in interstate carriers, they were primarily bacteriological, having in mind the prevention of hazard to health and of unpalatable water.[9] During revisions in 1925, 1942, 1946, and 1962, chemical and physical criteria were added. Bacteriological requirements were liberalized and then made more precise; restrictions on water softening were imposed and then relaxed. The fluoride limit was increased while the magnesium limit was reduced. In the case of criteria for human health as well as aquatic life and industrial, agricultural, and recreational uses, the criteria have changed as scientific research has yielded new understanding of the natural relationships involved or has permitted more precise measurements. Because of fluctuations in the flow and quality of natural waters, an effluent which would be objectionable at one time would be permissible at another, and because of advances in technology new potentially harmful effluents such as pesticides are added to streams faster than new methods of treating them are perfected. Wastes are regarded as being tolerable in terms of the damages they are perceived to cause and of judgment as to the practicability of preventing them. The chief variables in setting criteria for water quality therefore are the peculiar environment of the stream, the uses that could be made of it, the knowledge of biological, physical and social relationships between water quality and use, the technology of treating waste and water, and the values placed by society on different uses.

Against this background it may be argued that clean water is what the public agencies judge the articulate and influential citizen groups are willing to accept, given their perception of the costs and gains entailed.

Standards for Pollution Abatement

By the time of the National Resources Planning Board serious questions were raised about aspects of water quality other than public health— its effects upon recreation, wildlife management, and agriculture. The Board tried to give attention to these and followed the device of setting up an investigating committee, the Special Committee on Water Pollution which in a series of reports recommended steps for the federal government to take in collaboration with state agencies to refine thinking about water quality.[10] While these were not accepted on a wide scale, they represented the first serious examination of the spectrum of opinion about stream cleanliness, and they helped shape the thinking which the Public Health Service pursued in research and in its relations to state health agencies.

The research and public discussion came to fruition in the 1948 Water Pollution Control Act which for the first time gave legislative recognition to pollution as a national problem. The federal government took the initiative in developing comprehensive plans for pollution abatement in cooperation with the states, extended credit for construction of local waste treatment plants, and expanded its research and technical services. While the primary responsibility for controlling pollution remained with the states, a mild sort of federal enforcement was to be exercised with the consent of the state when state efforts had been exhausted.

The President's Water Resources Policy Commission turned its attention to the effectiveness of the water pollution control activities and proposed a trial period before regulation was to be considered, saying:

> If this Federal-State-local cooperative pollution-control program fails to provide the country with clean rivers within a period of 10 years, the 1948 Act should be reconsidered with a view to providing for Federal enforcement, without the requirement of State consent, where polluted streams are within the jurisdiction of Congress. (Vol. I, p. 195)

By 1956 it was plain that the streams were not being cleaned up, and new authorizations were made to give federal grants to support municipal waste treatment construction, to exercise enforcement on interstate streams, and to push ahead more vigorously with basin planning and with research. The pace of investment in sewage treatment plants approximately doubled during the next 10 years, and federal enforcement actions were taken in more than 30 instances, with notable effect along the Missouri River. But the advance still was slow by comparison with the rising flow of municipal and industrial waste.

By 1961 the Senate Select Committee had this to say about water pollution:

> Improvements in methods for dealing with pollution have not been extensive in the past several decades. Also, the Nation has lagged in building facilities for pollution abatement making use of

the techniques that are known. Progress has been made in cleaning up some streams, but the backlog of needs is still very large. As the demand for water grows, and as more widespread reuse of water becomes necessary, it will be essential for a great deal more progress to be made in the construction of sewage and industrial waste treatment works, and in regulation of the flow of rivers so that adequate quantities of dilution water will be available during periods of low flow. (pp. 12–13)

An influential shift in federal thinking about water pollution had come in a National Conference the preceding year.[11] This had been prepared with great care by the Public Health Service, working in collaboration with interested citizen groups, and it brought together diverse streams of thinking which provided sufficient clarification of agreement and disagreement to lay the groundwork for new and broader water pollution legislation by the Congress. This also gave sufficient impetus to the Congress so that it was better able to focus its concern for water pollution among its own committees.

Thereafter, two lines of scientific inquiry helped give definition to public thinking about water quality. One was the investigation by Kneese of the circumstances in which the private and social costs and benefits of pollution might be estimated and assessed.[12] The other was the canvass by a National Academy of Sciences committee of the whole range of environmental deterioration.[13] The same theme then was followed by a panel of the President's Science Advisory Committee.[14] The magnitude and social management of pollution now were seen more accurately.

The water pollution legislation of 1965 demonstrates a more resolute and unified kind of congressional responsibility. Stiffer enforcement powers were granted, the financial aid for municipal construction of waste treatment was stepped up, and the executive authority was focussed in a Federal Water Pollution Control Administration under the Secretary of the Interior. This did not centralize federal responsibility for dealing with water pollution any further than successive flood control acts had vested responsibility for flood problems in the Corps of Engineers. After a long period during which septic tanks and cesspools were progressively replaced by sewer systems, these systems had begun to proliferate in outlying urban areas. The federal mortgage guarantee agencies, urban planning agencies and highway planners were exercising major influence on the growth of urban housing and public utilities. The Public Health Service retained control over drinking water standards. The Corps of Engineers was the principal instrument for planning and constructing storage works which would affect the dilution capacity of streams. Land use planning and development for recreational, wildlife preservation, and agricultural purposes, of course, continued in other governmental hands.

As the new administration launched its field operations, it encountered great disparity in views as to relative values of water among the constituency. The flavor of diversity of view is suggested by the trouble the National Conference had encountered in defining clean water. Three separate panels brought in three statements as follows (emphasis added):[15]

Panel I   "We recommend that the Conference express its conviction that the goal of pollution abatement is to protect and enhance the capacity of the water resource to serve the widest possible range of human needs, and that this goal can be approached only by accepting the positive policy of keeping waters as *clean as possible,* as opposed to the negative policy of attempting to use the full capacity of water for waste assimilation."

Panel II   "(1) Users of water do not have an inherent right to pollute; (2) users of public waters have a responsibility for returning them as nearly *clean as technically possible;* and (3) prevention is just as important as control of pollution."

Panel III   "The national goal with respect to stream protection should be the safeguarding of water quality. Every stream should be made to provide for the *fullest range of uses for the type of society served,* and consistent with the variabilities within and among different river basins."

The difference of emphasis on what is "possible," "technically possible," and "the fullest range of uses for the type of society served" reveals the difference of judgment as to whether waste should be kept out of streams entirely or only to the extent consistent with particular stream characteristics and uses.

One of the significant benefits from application of computer technology to water resources systems is in its requirement that aims and standards be explicit and precise. The resulting specifics may be laid open to inspection, and the wisdom of setting a uniform standard may be ventilated by debate. Oftentimes the explicit statement of a criterion reveals how little is known of the biological and physical processes on which it is presumed to be based. Then the argument may turn to whether it is prudent to await the results of further research, as on virus indexes and pesticide toxicity, or to act promptly and perhaps unwarrantedly to curb an allegedly rising menace.

There is no point in examining here the immense intricacies of discovering natural relationships and the potentialities of technical action to alter them. The National Symposium at Ann Arbor in 1966 revealed many of those complexities. Rather, interest centers on two related problems: what devices can be used to carry out mutually consistent public programs and to resolve ambiguity within them, and what role the assessment of public attitudes has in such a search.

The Struggle for Mutually Consistent Programs

If each government agency concerned with water development were somehow to plan so as to take into account multiple aims and careful appraisal of the multiple means available to achieve those aims, there still would remain the problem of coordinating the administration of the many agencies involved. This probably is the most persistent problem involved in American water management. A large part of its history can be written around efforts to achieve coordination among federal and state agencies having somewhat different aims and employing somewhat different methods.

From the prescient speculations of the Inland Waterways Commission in 1908 through the activities of the still infant Water Resources Council in 1966 a chronic question has been "How can the nation obtain unified plans for water management without having a single unified agency?" A corollary question of whether unified plans are either desirable or attainable has received less attention. The Commission sought to resolve this emerging issue by recommending the establishment of an agency to correlate the programs of individual agencies, and Senator Newlands pushed for a Waterways Commission with that purpose. It was authorized but never appointed, and was eliminated with the Federal Water Power Act of 1920.

Under that Act the Federal Power Commission had the task of licensing construction of new non-federal water power projects on public lands and navigable streams and also of studying opportunities for development of power at storage sites by federal agencies. Although the study powers were rather broad, the Commission took a generally passive role so that when hydro-power generation became a major feature of new federal investment the agency exercised little initiative in promoting unified plans, and contented itself with licensing, advising on power facilities, and assessing downstream benefits.

It was not until the National Resources Board began operations in 1934 that a sustained effort was made to correlate the water plans of federal agencies. Three developments emphasized the need for such coordination. The Corps of Engineers had begun the issuance of "308" reports; the Tennessee Valley Authority had captured the imagination of the American people as a venture in integrated management of natural resources for human good; the Bureau of Reclamation had enlarged its activities to include flood control and hydro-power as well as irrigation.

The difficulty of correlating the Corps of Engineers and the Bureau of Reclamation and their work with that of other related agencies, such as state agencies concerned with recreational development and federal agencies concerned with forest conservation, soil conservation, and municipal and state public power marketing activities, came into prominence in reviewing the Public Works Administration projects proposed for federal support. In response to Congressional resolutions, President Roosevelt appointed the Secretaries of War, Agriculture, Interior, and Labor to bring in a comprehensive plan for development of the nation's rivers, and ten were selected for reporting. At the same time a Board of Review established by the Public Works Administrator saw the need for taking a comprehensive view of all proposed projects within the same basin. This led to the creation of the Mississippi Valley Committee and to its drafting a general plan for development of the Mississippi Valley in 1934. The Committee was composed of distinguished citizen members plus the Chief of Engineers. Its report was criticized as being not sufficiently detailed to permit early decision on construction plans, and also as neglecting considerations which would have been brought to bear by federal and state agencies had they shared in the undertaking.

The latter criticism was remedied when the Committee was converted into the Water Resources Committee of the National Resources Committee in 1934 by the addition of federal members from the Department of Agriculture, the Department of the Interior, the Public Health Service, and the Federal Power Commission. In its Drainage Basin Reports for 1936, revised in 1937, the Committee sought to bring forward coordinated study and construction programs for the country as a whole, taking into account both the aspirations and programs of federal agencies and of state agencies such as state sanitary engineers, state water engineers, and other groups represented through the newly created state planning boards.[16]

From the outset, the Water Resources Committee faced the problem of whether it simply would be an arm of the federal agencies or whether it would exercise some kind of independent judgment. In the event that two federal agencies had somewhat different plans for the same area the committee could endorse both, seek to achieve a compromise satisfactory to the two of them for the same area, or try to work out an independent solution which seemed more in the public interest. To do the latter would require independent staff. A reasonable reaction to the irritation provoked by conflicting views was to vest all authority in one agency, and the Congress in 1937 designated the Corps of Engineers as that agency by means of a joint resolution.

The presidential veto of Senate Joint Resolution 47 was a crucial step in the coordination struggle. Had President Roosevelt not blocked the Congressional intent, an action which he would have found exceedingly difficult to sustain without National Resources Committee drainage basin studies providing a standard to which other federal agencies could rally, the Corps of Engineers would have received the principal responsibility for bringing in comprehensive plans. A few years later the other agencies were strong enough in their demonstrated activity in water planning to defeat any such suggestion.

The experience of the National Resources Committee and its successor, the National Resources Planning Board, is being appraised by Lepawsky,[17] but it may be timely to suggest a few consequences so far as water resources management is concerned. Agencies were brought together for the first time to work not only across federal lines but in cooperation with state and local groups in assessing agency programs. A procedure was developed with support of the Bureau of the Budget by which plans proposed by one agency for water development were subject to review by other agencies prior to being sent to Congress (Executive Order No. 9384). Hard discussion among agency personnel over issues of policy and procedure was encouraged and often went far beyond the required formal exchanges. But the success of the National Resources Planning Board in those directions was counteracted by its challenging the authority of individual federal agencies to report directly to Congress and by resentment of congressmen and some state officials to a reviewing mechanism placed between them and the executing federal agency.

Following its abolition in 1943, certain of the significant contributions of the National Resources Planning Board in the water field continued to be administered through an informal interagency committee known as the Federal River Basin Committee. This, in turn, was succeeded by the Interagency Committee for Water Resources. Both provided a mechanism by which the staff of federal agencies could meet with each other to discuss prominent programs and policies. They carried out a number of useful activities such as the formulation of procedures for economic appraisal of water resources projects. They had no power to alter the activities of their member agencies, and they could move only so far as the policies and the personal good will of agency administrators would permit.

The first Hoover commission, confronted with this array of agencies having informal collaboration and participating somewhat reluctantly in Bureau of Budget review reports to Congress, proposed radical administrative reorganization.[18] The Task Force on Natural Resources suggested that there should be created a single federal water resources agency in which would be amalgamated the Corps of Engineers, the Bureau of Reclamation, and certain other federal agencies directly involved. The Commission itself proposed a somewhat different solution, but neither recommendation received the approval of the Congress. Although chairman Hoover was deeply committed to a mission, which he had conceived while Secretary of Commerce, to divest the Corps of Engineers of its civil functions, and although there had been strong support ten years earlier in special administrative studies for merging public works agencies under a single roof, the political climate was unfriendly to unification of water management agencies.

When the President's Water Resources Policy Commission moved into action in 1950 it explicitly excluded consideration of administrative arrangements in trying to carry out its task of reviewing policy. Administrative reorganization efforts were regarded as booby traps almost certain to ruin any attempted unification and harmonization of federal policy. Likewise, the President's Materials Policy Commission skated clear of organizational considerations in making its more superficial recommendations on water resources for industry and agriculture.

The next step was the creation by the President in 1954 of an Advisory Committee on Water Resources Policy made up of three cabinet officers with contributions by other agencies. Their report did not lead to any major changes in resources organization. The old battles continued and new ones developed.

The Senate Select Committee on National Water Resources likewise avoided changes in administrative organization of the federal agencies. It limited itself to recommending new lines of research and to suggesting the need for periodic assessment of the nation's water resources situation by some agency which would play the coordinating role which sixteen years before had rested with the National Resources Planning Board. The Senate Select Committee made remarkable contributions to the advancement of research on water and laid the groundwork for the creation of the Water Resources Council in 1965, an agency which is essentially a coordinating agency of responsible federal organizations.

All the while the specter of the Tennessee Valley Authority hung over considerations of agency collaboration. The threat of a Missouri Valley Authority clearly had been responsible for the regional wedding between the Bureau of Reclamation and the Corps of Engineers under which each agency, after bitter wrangling, endorsed the other's projects and thus precluded any third agency being introduced into the family situation. The valley authority alternative had been in the background of basin studies discussed in Chapter III.

By 1966 the most far-reaching proposal affecting federal organization was for the creation of a national water commission. This would be authorized over a period of five years to report on policies and procedures in the field of water resources and to draw to the extent it wished upon federal agencies for studies and participation. It was regarded in the words of Senator Jackson, its leading sponsor, as instructed to "study alternative solutions to water resources problems without prior commitment to any interest group, region or agency of government. The Commission will be charged with responsibility of reviewing water policy in the light of the broad national interest."[19] Thus, it would attempt to give a national perspective which presumably was lacking in the Water Resources Council.

Coordination, Agency Mission, and Public Preferences

Throughout this long attempt at coordinating water resources plans by federal agencies in collaboration with state and local agencies, two interpretative themes often appear. One theme is that the agencies can coordinate their efforts only to the extent that their policies are mutually consistent, and that because policies as given to them by the Congress and by the state legislatures are often inconsistent or divergent, it basically is impracticable for them to arrive conscientiously at coordinated plans: ambiguity fosters administrative confusion on the water front. The complementary theme is that inconsistency of policy is strengthened in many respects by agency rivalries, that empire building leads to divergent policies, that competing programs foster wider consideration of alternatives, and that the whole effort of administrative officers is to resist activities which would either submerge their independent responsibilities or merge agencies in a single water management agency with a common policy. Rather than developing fewer agencies through coordination of efforts, there has been a proliferation of independent and splinter agencies during a time when increased implications of water management have been widely recognized.

A somewhat different kind of interpretation is worth examining. It is that basic to the competitive and divergent activity of federal agencies is inconsistency of federal and state legislative policy, that the inconsistencies in legislative policy are to be traced to ambiguity on the part of the public as to what it wants from water management, and that this ambiguity tends to be fostered rather than resolved by the activities of individual federal agencies. The theme can be elaborated by returning to the experience with federal involvement in abatement of water pollution.

Wengert suggests that the traditional and proper mode for resolving ambiguity in public aims is in the democratic legislative process.[20] A technical engineer or forester in a government bureau cannot be expected to finally set values for trees or scenic views; these values exist only in the minds of the public. The public has its most direct expression through its elected legislative representatives. Under this view the resolution of ambiguity as to public ends and means takes place in the halls of Congress. However, many of the basic conflicts in aims and values do not necessarily emerge in reports to the legislature.

Devices for Resolving Ambiguity

In fact, the American people have used a wide variety of devices to attempt to resolve ambiguity or conflict when it arises at national or local levels. Confronted with the vagueness and diversity of standards for water quality, it may be helpful to ask what have been the merits of at least seven of these devices and whether any new forms are required.

A *standing committee of the Congress* may, in the course of its review of reports or investigation of problems brought before it, enunciate policy which will resolve questions of disparity in public aims. The complication here is that the committees of Congress traditionally are specialized. No one committee of the House or the Senate deals with water resources problems as a whole, as demonstrated by the necessity for the Senate to establish a special committee when it attempted to grasp the complexity involved in water management. Standing committees have, however, acted to resolve certain questions of ambiguity in public policy. They played a leading role in sorting out the responsibility for water pollution control, including the uncertainty as to its coming under the jurisdiction of fisheries, public works, or public health. A further example is that of the Public Works Committee of the House in revising policy with respect to federal investment in small flood control reservoirs involving both the Corps of Engineers and the Soil Conservation Service. This was a Solomon-like decision which gave each agency a part of the baby.[21]

Typically, a Congressional committee is confronted with either a recommendation from one agency of a particular plan or recommendations of a conflicting nature from two or more agencies operating in the same field. The tradition of engineering practice in water management is for the responsible investigating agency to bring forward a single plan and to request legislative approval or disapproval. There is no adequate mechanism for bringing to a Congressional committee a set of recommendations in which a range of alternatives is presented and in which the committee is given the opportunity to make the preliminary selection as to quality standards and means of reaching them rather than to rely upon the administrative judgment of the recommending agency. The fighting usually takes place before a report reaches the public gaze on the tables of a Congressional committee. In the case of Potomac pollution abatement plans in 1963 there was no precedent for bringing tentative statements of standards for discussion in advance of preparing a plan; the procedure may be considered a pioneer step in exploring alternatives.

A *special Congressional investigation* can be made to clarify ambiguity where it has not been possible to achieve this through a standing committee. The Senate Select Committee on National Water Resources is an outstanding example of this insofar as assessment of the national water situation is concerned. In commissioning the Wollman study of water needs and in using the resulting estimates in its report, the Select Committee brought about a momentous shift in technical and public thinking about water quality, for it gave wide publicity to the view that a massive increase in stream flow storage would be required to meet the nation's future needs for waste dilution. The stage was set for planning basin programs for construction of storage works in contrast to advanced waste treatment or to readjustment in land uses.

Even though such investigations may be farmed out to consultants, as in the case of the water use study, or to an agency, as in the case of the flood insurance study, they receive respectful consideration by the Congress and their record of translating findings into action seems better than for similar studies set up in the Executive Branch. The insurance study was distinguished in that it undertook a systematic examination of public preferences, using an opinion survey procedure to estimate receptivity of flood plain occupants to insurance were it to be offered.[22]

The Select Committee itself in holding a series of regional hearings on water problems tried to elicit opinion from various sectors of water managers and stirred up interest in its activities.

Special investigations launched under the aegis of the executive, usually with the knowledge of the Congress but without specific legislative authorization, have not been tried for water quality problems. Examples from other sectors of water management are the series of reclamation fact-finders reports, the special panel appointed by the Secretary of the Interior to deal with the evaluation of secondary benefits from reclamation projects,[23] and the special board appointed by the Bureau of Budget to recommend revised standards for economic evaluation of water projects.[24] In such cases it appears that the success of the venture depends not only upon the quality of those who carry it out but on the rightness of the timing, and unless it enjoys strong support from both legislative and executive sides it may have little effect on policy.

Without setting up an elaborate investigation, the executive may enunciate unified policies drawing upon the experience and judgment of the agencies, and expecting Congressional assent. This has not been tried for water quality aims. Reference already has been made to its use in developing a unified program of management of flood losses.

A more common device is that of the *Presidential commission,* with or without Congressional sponsorship, which has larger powers, takes more time, and subjects its findings to a broader array of public discussion and debate. Examples of this are the Inland Waterways Commission, the National Reclamation Commission, the two Hoover Commissions, the President's Water Resources Policy Commission, the Missouri River Commission, the Southeast River Basins Commission, and the Texas Basins Commission.

Several of these have received careful appraisal,[25] but it may be useful to note certain aspects of their experience bearing on clarification of policy and procedures. They often have greater impact upon public action through their influence upon the quality of public thinking on the issues involved than through translation of their recommendations into federal legislation or procedures. Thus, although a substantial number of the specific recommendations by the President's Water Resources Policy Commission in 1950 were carried into action through the intermediary of a special committee established by the Director of the Bureau of the Budget leading to Circular A–47, the Commission's longer-term impact probably was in its effect upon public discussion of the prospect for federal water quality enforcement and of the need for improved procedures for evaluation of federal investment.

Commission recommendations are more likely to gain acceptance if they have the prior and enthusiastic approval of federal agencies. Without such approval, even though there is no strenuous opposition, the ideas tend to be buried, and agency involvement in the study shows itself later in the attention it draws to the findings. Indeed, where in conflict with strongly held views of principal federal agencies, commission recommendations receive relatively little attention and are unlikely to be translated into legislative action.

Probably a major disadvantage of a Presidential commission is its lack of direct involvement of members of the Congress. In this respect it is important to note that the Outdoor Recreation Resources Review Commission and the Public Lands Law Review Commission had representation from the Congress, whereas the proposed Water Resource Commission would be composed exclusively of people from outside federal employment. Where Congressional action inevitably will be called for as in the case of regional allocations of water of specified quality, it would be desirable to provide for Senate and House participation from the outset.

National conferences offer one illuminating way of clarifying public opinion as to values involved in water management. The 1960 Water Pollution Conference clearly went far toward defining the issues. The 1966 Symposium on Standards sharpened technical thinking as to criteria.[26] Poorly prepared and unsupported by systematic cultivation of the interested citizen groups, as was the White House Conference on Conservation in 1964, conferences can have little or no influence. Prepared carefully over a sufficient period of time, as was the White House Conference on Natural Beauty in 1965, they can make a major impact upon policy. At times like icebergs, their bulk lies beneath the surface of the visible conference, but unlike icebergs there is no recognized relation between the visible and invisible volumes.

Independent study and assessment by non-government agencies may help resolve public confusion and has had a profound effect upon thinking about ways of maintaining water quality. Under the auspices of Resources for the Future, Kneese's work on economic implications of water quality went far to stimulate thoughtful investigation of the social costs and benefits of clean water and of practicable methods of sharing the costs.[27] Similarly, Davis' study of the Potomac straightened out a good deal of the popular confusion as to whether the only way to prevent further degradation of the lower river's quality was through additional storage reservoirs.[28] The Harvard Water Resources Seminar contributed a whole new set of insights into the issues involved in multiple-purpose management. It is remarkable that the federal agencies had not been able to organize inquiries of that character, and it seems likely that where the probing of public issues is linked with refinement of measures for recognizing the forces involved, the non-government agency has heavy advantages.

The government agencies are never quite certain how far they should go or can go in using a device which sets out to cope with diversity in public preference by consciously molding it. This is *public information and education.* Applied in a gingerly fashion by agencies fearing legislative criticism of their influencing legislation, the information programs do affect the articulation of value judgments to an unknown but probably significant degree.

When the Public Health Service was faced with administering the 1948 water pollution control policy it published statements of the clean streams problem and of its program which inescapably suggested the proper lines of federal action and which avoided a head-on debate over expanding federal enforcement by quoting the President's Water Resources Policy Commission.[29] After ten years of experimentation with the program as expanded in 1956, the Service was easier in describing activities but more restrained in directly implying that radical changes in policy were in order.[30] At this point the National Conference had been sponsored, and the Service became the medium for disseminating what others said about weaknesses in statements of aims and means but was torn by argument as to whether pollution abatement should remain under the Service or be given new identity in the Department of the Interior.

All of these devices have in some degree the purpose of clarifying aims and of helping set policy as to relative values of resources and resource uses. As indicated earlier, an alternative approach may be to eschew more detailed policy statements and to let standards or project design be set by field study methods in which there is conscious effort to sound out the prevailing public attitudes toward water and land resources in a particular area. To do so implies that public attitudes are not haphazard and that techniques are available for sounding them so as to find out their regularities.

Attitudes Toward Environmental Quality

Attitudes held by individuals toward the natural environment and sectors of it appear to vary according to the experience which the individual has had with the environment and according to personality traits which, in turn, are partly the product of his total environmental experience.[31] It is known that these vary from time to time within limits set by physical conditions or social orientation. They are subject to modest change according to experience and information which is made available to the people concerned. There cannot be said to be universal standards of natural beauty or of judgment of natural quality of environment: these are relative and may be transitory. Thus, with water quality, as with views toward landscape or the hazard of drought, it can be expected that attitudes will differ over both space and time, and that they can be identified.

The simple solicitation of an opinion from an individual about the condition of a stream may mean little in terms of his preferences unless he is presented with viable and realistic alternatives among which he can express a preference. To say that a person who states he would like to have a reservoir used for fishing has this as his first preference when he has not been given an understanding of the other options which might be open for the use of the reservoir tells us little about the real judgment which the person would exercise in a situation in which the choice did exist.

In certain situations the response may be influenced by the person's sense of efficacy. The citizen may be less likely to press for reducing pollutants if he is told that there is no way of eliminating them, but this, too, probably varies with personal orientation and the extent to which the individual regards himself as relating to tasks or to people. Some may shrink from the avowedly impossible while others attack it with zest.

The attitude which any one person or group may have can be ascertained in several ways. Man's perception of environmental stimuli, such as his response to a natural stream, can be inferred from his literary expressions, and by interview. His sense of the severity of a pollution problem can be identified by interview. His disposition to take action about it can be judged both by his responses and by laboratory situations. These can be examined in relation to the individual's broad value orientations and to the situation of political and inter-personal relations in which choice is exercised. Where there is opportunity to let the consumer make his choice in a free market, as when he has open to him the purchase of camping facilities on a variety of lakes having different characteristics of water quality and fishing, the most accurate judgments can be formed as to the values he assigns to quality. The circumstances where this is possible are restricted by lack of user charges for many water facilities and by the few choices available. Shadow pricing, which measures values in lieu of market prices, can offset these drawbacks in part.[32] Even if it were practicable to establish a system of effluent charges for a nation's waters, a scheme which on both economic and administrative grounds would seem wiser than a program of enforcing standards and financing new construction, there would remain the question of the basic criteria of stream cleanliness on which charges would be based.

Public tolerance or intolerance of stream conditions may be expected to change in response to new technologies and to new views of the practicable. Just as one of the profound shifts in attitudes toward stream cleanliness came with the Senate Select Committee estimates of dilution possibilities, a further adjustment in view as to what is clean water and which uses of it should be favored may be expected as sectors of the public become convinced of the efficacy of new forms of waste treatment or river management. The adventures in space travel, however short they may fall of locating well-watered havens on the moon, may have a momentous effect upon water management. The Argonauts in satellites live on a closed system of water which is ingested, voided, treated, and used again without apparent offense to health, taste, or aesthetics. To the extent that the methods for reuse on a larger scale are perfected and that the consuming public views them as acceptable, the stage is set for wide adoption of reuse systems for individual houses as well as entire cities. The principal obstacle is alleged public resistance to drinking re-used water.

While the biological, physical, and chemical characteristics of streams are monitored with considerable precision, the nature of human perception of them and aspirations for their use is assessed casually and at best crudely.

Agency Sounding of Public Preferences

State and federal agencies take soundings of public preferences by three major devices. The most structured and probably the least fruitful is the scheduled public hearing which either at the outset or near the end of a field study invites the interested local groups to come forward in a public forum and present their views as to the problems and their possible solutions, often being led by local legislators who demonstrate their interest in the right outcome. The Federal Water Pollution Control Administration arranges such hearings when a comprehensive basin study is being organized and when specific enforcement complaints have been drawn up. Like the standard procedure of the Corps of Engineers, all potentially concerned citizen groups are notified of the time and place, given time to speak, questioned where appropriate, and duly recorded.

A second method is the hearing held by Congressional committees and special commissions in passing upon agency budget recommendations or in weighing the need for legislative action. These hearings often consist of a routine presentation of a project followed by miscellaneous remarks of whatever legislators and group representatives are sufficiently involved to make an appearance. When, however, a committee staff takes the trouble to pose specific questions and to seek particular types of witnesses, as when Senator Muskie and Representative Blatnik organized inquiries into the need for revised pollution abatement legislation or when the Senate Select Committee on National Water Resources set out to canvass the prevailing views as to water quality, hearings become a means of not only drawing judgments as to public opinion but of shaping its expression. The kinds of questions asked and the people testifying influence the thinking of editorial writers, commentators, and other representatives who might not otherwise be inclined to take a stand.

Notwithstanding the formal hearings, there can be little doubt that the sources of public preference on which planners place the greater reliance are the informal expressions coming from professional associates and friends, the personal judgments of what citizens groups want or will reject, the intimate assessment of how far a regulation can go without provoking retaliation or what will please the dollar-minded municipal council while placating the wildlife enthusiasts. Rarely recorded and rarely presented in public documents, this sounding of preferences goes far toward shaping the assumptions as to what the public wants that are imbedded, often beneath the surface, in plans for managing water quality. These may be critical assumptions that the water consumers will not take water from a reservoir where boating is permitted or that dissolved oxygen downstream from a treatment plant must be sufficient to permit shad to flourish.

Just how accurate these assessments of public preference may be is not often tested, for the common test is whether or not a plan based upon them meets with formal approval by the municipal, state, or federal authority concerned. Such approval cannot be taken as unqualified confirmation of preferences. As has been shown, the valid test is when the citizen is presented with a full range of choice in circumstances which give him an accurate sense of the efficacy of each course of action. A public opinion survey may go part of the way toward an accurate sounding.

The Outdoor Recreation Resources Review Commission was the first Federal agency to make serious use of opinion survey techniques to arrive at judgments as to what the public wanted from natural resources.[33] Using the University of Michigan Survey Research Center, the Commission did find out how people responded to questions as to how they currently enjoyed the outdoors and what preferences they thought they had as to its uses in the future. The findings played a significant role in the judgments which the Commission made as to types of public programs to be initiated or supported.

For the most part, however, federal as well as state administrators continue to rely upon their own personal judgment. Because of their practical experience with the way in which consumers behave at public parks, or the response of the irrigators to a water use contract, or the reaction of the municipal councils to rate schedules offered by public power marketing agencies, administrators usually simplify issues by offering the public the choice of accepting or rejecting a concrete proposal.

Except for those hearings which turn on proposals being hotly contested, as when a city official considers a waste treatment enforcement order to be unjust and technically faulty, these procedures rarely expose the full set of possible solutions in a situation which either provides information about them or encourages relatively dispassionate appraisal. Opinion surveys have not yet attempted to do so. Hearings held at the outset of a planning study tend to solicit opinions in such a loose framework that they elicit only those ideas that are well formed or are enthusiastically iconoclastic. Public discussion of reports presenting definite recommendations may draw healthy fire and sometimes lead to changes in design or to public opposition which kills the proposal, but they do not often consider the many assumptions as to public preference which are plowed into the engineering design and they do not explicitly call for review of the other opportunities. Even when the Corps of Engineers made a heroic effort to present the range of choice for curbing pollution in the lower Potomac it did so by giving different storage schemes to maintain the dissolved oxygen of the estuary water at a certain assumed level.[34] Davis in his survey of the same problem showed that there were many other means deserving appraisal, such as advanced treatment, sewage diversion, oxygenation, and hundreds of combinations thereof, and that the assumed criterion of quality was itself subject to question.[35]

From the variety of methods of measuring public preferences for water quality has come the strong conviction that stream pollution should be halted, but no very clear leading as to what uses should be preferred and how much the public is willing to sacrifice to enforce more demanding criteria.

Toward a More Sensitive Assessment

If the essentially relative and transitory character of public judgments about quality of environment are to be heeded, it will be important to set standards that can shift over time and vary from one environment to another, and to determine those preferences in a systematic and sound fashion. This would imply moving toward more flexible standards with wider and more frequent consultation with the public groups involved, as exemplified by the Outdoor Recreation Resources Review Commission. A conference like the National Conference on Water Pollution might become a recurring exercise on both the national and the regional scale for the assessment and reappraisal of public opinions as to valuation of the environment.

Another concrete way of fulfilling these conditions would be for a federal agency such as the Federal Water Pollution Control Administration to energetically experiment with a refined hearing procedure that would seek representative samples of resource users, and would provide them with information as to the full range of alternatives in circumstances which would permit a thoughtful value judgment unfettered by alignment for or against a particular project. This would elicit preferences which could be appraised systematically. It would test the usual assumptions more rigorously, and it inevitably would alter the attitudes themselves. Indeed, one danger might be the temptation to rig the apparently objective hearing so as to build support for a conclusion the sponsoring agency favored. An incidental but highly significant part of such an exercise would be to identify the biases and values of the administrators involved. Whether sharpened by conference or hearing, the new expression of preference would affect political decision as to policy and standards.

Two general conclusions emerge from review of federal experience in finding out the public's wants with respect to water quality.

The distinction between finding what the public wants and guiding the public in the forming of preferences is essentially in the individual administrator's view of public service. Legislative guides are silent on the right procedure. For the administrator who knows what the public ought to have or who instinctively feels he knows its preferences, the simplest solution is to give it only one choice and to accept the response as confirming or denying that judgment. For the administrator who earnestly seeks to discover what the public prefers, the road is rougher and the way is not well marked. It calls for experiments with methods of measuring the public values and their variations, and doing so before rather than after a definite plan has been formulated. It avoids presenting a take-it-or-leave-it choice until there has been a searching canvass of what the public will take.

Second, it is important to remember that asking for preference is meaningful only if a valid range of choice is presented in a framework that offers efficacious action. It is not enough to present a theoretical range: the range must be one which the individual feels is available to him and with respect to which he has the capability to act. Assessment must take place before definite plans have been drawn. In making it, there should be candid recognition that the methods employed may shape the results, and that the preferences may vary over time and space.

Standards of what constitutes clean water may be expected to shift in the years ahead. As more water uses take shape and as the technology for water management advances, the number of practicable ways of meeting human demands will increase while the demands themselves multiply. More special interest groups—ranging from industry to conservators of natural beauty—will express preferences for water quality. The larger the number of alternatives and the faster the technological change, the less permanent will be the group preferences, and the larger the interest groups the less homogeneous their expression. Ambiguity of public aims in coping with water pollution seems bound to increase. The pattern of setting regional standards in relation to local stream conditions and human preferences seems the most promising avenue now open, but it will require much more refined assessment of what people want.

To a large degree the outcome will hinge upon how the local preferences are gauged. A reliable sounding of preferences requires that the citizen feel himself in a situation where conditions of choice are similar to those he will encounter in dealing with a real stream, that he be exposed to the full range of information and opinion as to the alternatives open to him, and that he have a realistic sense of man's capacity to deal with water and the life it sustains. To do this will call for a close and unprecedented collaboration of natural scientists and engineers with social scientists in designing a new kind of assessment that will inevitably change attitudes as it tests them. This is one of the exciting challenges lying ahead in water management.

Research as a Tool:
Timid Confirmation and the Long Leap

V

If science and its accompanying technology continue to advance at an accelerating pace, it would behoove any new water planning to take account of scientific investigation in anticipating future needs and solutions, and to use technological capacity to forge new solutions. Yet, research has been the tool most conspicuously neglected in the whole kit of instruments used in managing water in the United States. This is ironic because it reflects lack of faith in the science which made possible the technology on which much water management has proceeded over the decades. But it is a hard fact that the largest single agency construct-ing water projects, the Corps of Engineers, had no significant research activities other than hydraulic river models until a few years ago and lacked budget allocations permitting it to support basic investigations on water problems. The Bureau of Reclamation engages in research chiefly to assist in handling technical problems of dam, spillway, and canal design and of using soils under irrigation. It carries on modest study of the impact of irrigation on the economy and gives little atten-tion to alternative ways of achieving stabilization of crop production in dry areas.

Few who contemplate the bleak inaction of a railroad station which 50 years before was bustling with traffic or the bucolic calm of an inland canal which 100 years earlier was the object of energetic state promotion can escape at least a fleeting question as to whether the noble dams now being planned for 50 to 100 years ahead may not be similarly obsolete before those horizons are reached. Will later historians look back on the 1960's as the time when the great dam building reached its zenith? Will the resulting network of reservoirs and canals then seem antique monu-ments like Roman aqueducts in the landscape of Provence? Greater attention to applications of science and technology might anticipate this obsolescence in part, and, in any event, might make society better able to cope with obsolescence as it comes.

Research is just entering onto the scene as a major instrument of water management. At this crucial time it may be useful to assess three major efforts in the use of research for which there now is record of performance. The three are chosen for their diversity, and, taken together, they are not representative of the whole body of water research which includes parts of water chemistry, hydrology, hydraulics, agronomy, civil engineering, economics, geography, political science, and other related disciplines. They nevertheless illustrate three sustained public attempts to use research as a tool. One is the investigation of relations between land and vegetation, an essentially timid venture by the Department of Agriculture, as confirming relationships believed by field workers to exist. The second is the set of investigations into weather modification possibilities, a long leap undertaken, not without qualms and hesitation, by the National Science Foundation beginning in 1957. The third is the massive attempt under the Department of the Interior to improve methods of desalting sea water, also a long leap in terms of the public claims made in its behalf.

Vegetation and Stream Flow

One of the widespread and erroneous myths permeating popular thinking about water management in the United States is that there is a direct, invariable, and positive relationship between forest growth and stream flow. This was at the root of the passage of the Weeks Act in 1911 which for the first time authorized the federal government through the Forest Service to acquire lands beyond those already held in public ownership and not yet appropriated. The Weeks Act was based upon the view that forests affect the flow of water in streams, particularly low water flow, and thereby have a significant effect upon navigation possibilities, and that because of the government's responsibility for the regulation of commerce among states it should so manage upstream land as to affect the flow of water in interstate streams.

Given the myth as accepted by the Congress and given the broad concern which the foresters have shown for the management of forest lands for multiple purposes, it is instructive to examine the nature and consequences of research on vegetation and stream flow. Such questions as the relations between flood plain use and land use elsewhere or the relations between the watershed vegetation and the use of the land on which it grows may be excluded. An important part of the record is reviewed in Schiff's study of Forest Service attitudes toward problems of fire and water.[1]

The first and historic venture in measuring vegetation-stream flow relations was undertaken in the Upper Rio Grande Basin by the

Weather Bureau in cooperation with the Forest Service in order to demonstrate what was thought to be fact in passage of the Weeks Act.[2] The experimental procedure was superficially simple but endowed with exasperating complexities. Two small drainage areas in the neighborhood of Wagon Wheel Gap were set aside for observation. After a time for calibration, one was cleared of its timber, the other remained in a fine, mature stand. Rainfall and runoff in the drainage area were measured throughout.

The hydrologic results have been reported by Hoyt and Troxell,[3] but the moral has been mute. As several years of observations unfolded it began to be apparent that the runoff from the watershed in which the trees had been removed was not conspicuously less in the dry season or larger in the flood season than the runoff from the other drainage area. It began to be suspected that the total runoff was somewhat larger, but even more complicated factors other than forest management seemed to obscure and make extremely difficult the sort of generalizations which were presumed under the Weeks Act. For example, it was found that differences in the geological structure of the area generated amounts of watershed leakage that masked minor differences in stream flow resulting from the evaporation and transpiration from the soil surface. Although the effects of forest cover in curbing soil destruction were rather clear, by 1926 the effects on stream flow remained cloudy at best. Interest in the Wagon Wheel Gap experiment lagged and the experiment finally was abandoned.

There followed a period of years in which much was said but little was done about verifying watershed vegetation-runoff relationships. As noted in Chapter III, in the heat of the controversy over Lower Mississippi flood control sweeping assertions were made as to the effects of land use upon downstream flow and modest studies were organized, chiefly on small plots, to test those conclusions. Following the passage of the Soil Conservation Act in 1933 and the revigoration of forest activities in the same phase of the New Deal, new sets of experimental watersheds were initiated in the Department of Agriculture by agencies of high professional integrity. Small areas of less than 5 acres were set aside in pairs for different land treatment or were subjected to replicated treatments in a series, and measurements made at runoff and sediment movement as at Bethany, Missouri.[4] In order to get more accurate information on critical magnitudes of flood flows and water yields for purposes of designing small engineering structures, "typical watersheds" of 25 to 250 acres were established in regions having relatively uniform soil, terrain, and climatic conditions. By the mid 1930's several more

elaborate research stations were established to combine the other type
of study with more precise measurements of land and water parameters.
Such stations as that at Coshocton, Ohio, were similar in design to ones
established in the same period by the Forest Service at Coweeta, North
Carolina; Farmington, Utah; and San Dimas, California.[5] Careful observations were made of precipitation, temperature, wind, runoff, soil
moisture, water surface evaporation, transpiration, infiltration rates,
sediment load, and many related factors. At a later date, the Tennessee
Valley Authority instituted several experimental watershed measurements, principally in the Beech Basin of Tennessee.[6]

The watershed experiments were undertaken by competent scientific personnel in agencies fully committed to programs of managing
upstream soil and vegetation in the interest of downstream flow as well
as for the yield from the land itself. Even though there were only a few
years of record, the heads of the Soil Conservation Service and the Forest
Service in 1936 were so certain about the relationships involved that they
strongly advised the President it would be undesirable to undertake any
major flood control work along the Ohio River unless provision also were
made for managing land use upstream. Such arguments provoked strenuous objections from the engineering fraternity that were mediated in
part by a National Resources Committee group which gained agreement
to a little publicized but momentous judgment that land measures were
not sufficiently certain to warrant any modification in the design of downstream engineering works.[7] Public claims for vegetation as a substitute
for engineering were toned down. The earlier public assertions should
be recognized because they were made by individuals who in passing
on budgets and appointing personnel in their respective agencies were
on the one hand committed to experiments which might prove or dis-
prove the assumed basic relationships and on the other hand were seeking greater precision in designing land management activities.

The Soil Conservation Service and Forest Service watersheds turned
out to be elaborate, expensive, and conscientious ventures at measuring
what were regarded as important parameters of water behavior within
relatively small areas. Each watershed was equipped with the most
precise measuring instruments that could be found at the time. Efforts
were made to develop new and more precise measurements. Experimental inquiry was directed at requisite density and location of gauges,
new types of lysimeters for the measurement of evapotranspiration were
tried, means of measuring soil moisture and flow of water through the
soil were improved. The watershed areas were not in a strict sense
demonstration, they were experimental. They were dedicated to finding

out more precisely the relationship between the changing vegetative cover of a piece of land and the water behavior in that land and downstream. The whole thrust was to elaborate those relationships. Where an essential element in the set of relationships was understood only imperfectly or could not be measured accurately every effort was made to infer whatever relationship existed. This was the case with evapotranspiration for which there are still no genuinely adequate and practicable measurements over large land areas. It also was the case with respect to soil moisture; the methods are subject to high degree of error and are affected by the measuring process itself. Little attention was given to aspects not susceptible to management through land use and vegetation manipulation: for example, to the conditions of repressing evaporation from water surfaces.

The experience of the United States was not unique. As shown by the recent appraisal of watershed experimentation around the world sponsored by the International Association for Scientific Hydrology, other countries such as France, Australia, Hungary, and Italy became involved in somewhat similar ventures at the same time.[8] Some of them preceded the American experiments,[9] many of them are inspired by activities in the United States.

But the consequences were sobering. Gradually it became evident that there was not sufficient understanding of basic relationships among precipitation, evapotranspiration, water movement in the soil, and water movement in the stream to permit clear-cut generalizations about the effect of altering a parameter of land use or vegetation.[10] Certain measurements, such as those of evaporation and of soil moisture, were found to be subject to so much error and variance that generalizations over even small watershed areas were found to be extremely difficult. While certain concrete empirical guides to hydrologic aspects of watershed planning were developed, literally carloads of data from observation points in the experimental watersheds were collected by the two agencies with few meaningful conclusions emerging.

This general orientation continued until in 1959 a radical change was made in the organization of the Department of Agriculture. The Agricultural Research Service was set up with responsibility for carrying out research quite independent of the operations of the Soil Conservation Service and the Forest Service, and reexamination of the watershed experiments began. Over a period of time this led to slow abandonment of larger watersheds in some areas and to a reorientation of work in other areas. Attention turned more directly to understanding the fundamental equations of water balance and sediment movement; and without giving up the observations needed for spillway, dam, and ditch design, it concentrated on fewer, critical problems. Collaboration among biologists, geologists, hydrologists, and soil scientists was encouraged.[11] The synthesis of findings began to take place on university computers and in theoretical formulations.

The research now going on under the Agricultural Research Service and the Forest Service is not seeking timidly to confirm the desirability of operation agency programs. It is directed more frankly and systematically at understanding the basic relationships which continue to baffle man. The difference in emphasis highlights the difficulty of pursuing research which is essentially confirmatory. Studies of the type developed at Wagon Wheel Gap tend to abandon lines of investigation which yield negative results so far as the operating programs are concerned. They are tempted to ignore fruitful alternatives if those alternatives do not fall within the programs of the agencies. They look for effects rather than causes. It is difficult to say that the watershed experimental research exercised significant influence upon operations of the two agencies other than in specifying details of engineering design and in throwing a kind of enervating blanket over enthusiastic claims for their activities. Research has neither provided significant new measures nor suggested major modifications of old ones.

Weather Modification

Weather modification research is an opposite approach. It is a conscious, sometimes cautious, frequently criticized, and often controversial long leap in which faith is placed on research as holding opportunity to develop a new form of water management in the American economy.

Here, too, there is a myth with which the scientist has to contend. The Timber Culture Act of 1873 stated the conviction of the United States Congress that the growth of vegetation had a significant effect upon precipitation. So convinced was the Congress that it authorized the disposal of additional amounts of land in the Great Plains, particularly Nebraska, in order to encourage the settlers to plant trees. These were supposed to increase rainfall, render the land more suitable for permanent cultivation, and thereby enhance the transformation of the great American desert into a great American oasis. To this day the notion prevails that trees give off more moisture than grass and therefore cause more moisture to fall nearby. The same idea is implicit in the belief that building a reservoir or planting a shelter belt will change the climate across the Great Plains. The shelter belt operation of the 1930's did of course have significant effects upon local microclimates, and reservoirs may alter weather along their shores, but their effects upon broader climatic conditions have yet to be demonstrated.

Belief in weather modification is not new to the American public. Nevertheless, it was not until the late 1940's following on the Vonnegut experiments with ice nuclei that Sheafer and Langmuir's cloud chamber experiments made people think seriously about the possibility of altering some aspect of the weather by mechanical means. Speculations about the possibilities of cloud seeding with silver iodide or carbon dioxide set off a rash of commercial cloud seeding and government agitation and led to appointment of the President's Advisory Committee on Weather Control. Its report in 1957 presented evidence as to the possibility of cloud seeding and other forms of weather modification and recommended that a federal agency be given responsibility for sponsoring research in that field.[12]

The National Science Foundation responded with caution to the subsequent Congressional directive to support research. Its caution was conditioned in part by the chorus of critical discussion among statisticians who questioned the control situations and the interpretation of seeding data used by the Advisory Committee and in part by the slight attention given exploration of economic and social consequences of weather modification. These factors discouraged participation in further research by the academic community. The National Science Foundation found it was able to support all reasonably responsible research proposals that were presented in the field of weather modification. The most significant ones were those to determine the actual nature of precipitation, a process which is still not understood with precision. As commercial operations spread and as some of the experiments began to give more encouraging results, there were murmurings from Congress as to need for federal engagement in cloud seeding. When the Weather Bureau in high scientific detachment threw cold water on such proposals, the Congress found the Bureau of Reclamation not entirely unwilling to experiment in areas where drought and overestimation of available supplies had left the Bureau with projects short of water. As soon as the Bureau began to show an interest in cloud seeding and accepted its first million dollar appropriation from the House in 1965 for experiments in the Colorado Basin, the Weather Bureau began to feel it should have a hand in such activities, and the National Science Foundation questioned whether or not it had gone far enough and fast enough in promoting research in this direction. Such doubts led to the appointment by the National Science Foundation of a Special Commission on Weather Modification as well as to the organization by the National

Academy of Sciences-National Research Council of a special panel on the same subject.

The two groups submitted reports almost simultaneously in January, 1966, and provided the basis for wide public and Congressional discussion of the next steps in probing ways of changing climate and weather.[13] In anticipation of their reports, the Weather Bureau, newly transformed into the Environmental Science Services Administration, contributed its own estimate of the situation along with recommendations of ways in which its activities should be expanded and enhanced.[14] The three reports may be regarded as complementary. The Panel emphasized physical knowledge and possibilities. The Commission reviewed the field but went far in canvassing social, biological, and economic consequences and in suggesting implications for legal and administrative action. The Weather Bureau called attention to the relation of weather modification to the operations and research of the bureau charged with weather prediction and with understanding weather systems. The third no doubt was largely inspired by the emergence of the first two, which, in turn, had much stimulation from the Bureau of Reclamation action.

All three groups found modest possibility for weather modification over local areas as of early 1966, and saw some prospects for larger scale modification in the offing. They estimated the probability of there being an enlargement in man's capacity to modify the weather as sufficiently great to warrant action by public agencies to anticipate likely effects and to organize enlarged scientific research and technical capacity. The very exciting aspects of weather modification prospects are not so much the prospect of increases of the order of 10-15 percent in mean annual rainfall in an area of orographic precipitation, or of punching holes in super-cooled fog over airports with a high degree of certainty, or of suppressing hail over Great Plains wheat fields, or even of reducing by some significant proportion the number of lightning strikes in a tinder-dry forest area. They lie in the possibility of changing the pattern of atmospheric circulation and thus affecting precipitation or temperature over large regions, as well as in dealing with catastrophic situations such as the routes of tropical hurricanes or the distribution of short-period intense rainfall.

The Commission emphasized the importance of understanding the interrelated systems which would be affected by modification in the atmospheric system, these being not only the atmospheric system itself, for the rain shadow effects are not certain, but biological ecosystems, the hydrologic cycle, and the systems of production and communication which man has developed in relation to the hydrologic and biological conditions. Some ecologists, given the complexity and uncertainty of these relationships, counselled no further activity in weather modification until the relationships could be firmly established,[15] others pressed for more intensive investigations in the belief that modification would take place whether or not the full consequences were recognized and that the sooner they were anticipated the better.

The question is open as to how far the federal government can expect to go in advancing weather modification as a technique of water management for economic efficiency as well as for other social purposes. Clearly, it has responsibility to be alert to the need for public regulation of modification measures as they take shape from the standpoint of their effects on human activity and on opportunities to conduct further research. It also is evident that the federal government should guide whatever cooperation may be required with other countries. To the extent that manipulation is achieved over large areas, operations and control would need to be international.

The probing of basic physical, hydrologic, and biological relationships in their social context raises the issue of how much responsibility an operating agency such as the Bureau of Reclamation or the Army-Air Force should have for scientific research. The Bureau operations in the Colorado basin area during 1966 were justified largely in terms of their being experimental and contributing to scientific knowledge: no claims were made as to volume of change in water supply. The Weather Bureau justifies its involvement on the ground that it not only carries out basic research about weather but operates weather prediction centers. From the experience with vegetation-water relationships in the Department of Agriculture, a strong case can be made for separation under the administrative tent. In the Department of the Interior, the U.S. Geological Survey succeeds, but not without occasional departmental tension, in carrying out basic data collection and research functions independent of the operating function of agencies managing water. Similar division of responsibility for research on weather and for its application seems practicable.

Where should the responsibility rest for developing new techniques? One of the principal complications is the unwillingness of officials to take responsibility for hazardous ventures in new methods of weather modification. They not only risk a sense of failure but the taunts of competing agencies and the repercussions resulting from having oversold the possibility of a given device. There is less risk when a conscientious engineer undertakes to build a dam; he has the whole profession's experience in wise design and he is able to predict with reasonable confidence what the results will be so far as water storage is concerned, although not for many other aspects of dam construction. When he talks about a new device for increasing rainfall or suppressing hail or reducing lightning he runs the danger of jeopardizing his own reputation and the standing of his agency. If he can justify it as being a kind of research enterprise which might have practical benefits he is in a safer position, and this has been the case with the Bureau of Reclamation and cloud seeding in the Colorado Basin.

For this reason international efforts in weather modification may be especially significant at this stage. Not only might they assure genuine international use of the results for peaceful rather than belligerent purposes but international collaboration in weather modification research might serve to buoy up those who take the risk of the long leap. In place of the frenetic competition to get to the moon there can be collaboration in which the stakes are even higher in terms of consequences for mankind, and in which the responsibility is sufficiently spread over several nations and several disciplines that failure to achieve immediate results in one quarter does not necessarily bring down public wrath or budgetary cuts on the responsible agency.

Desalting

In only one other field of water management is there heavy systematic investment in research to expand the available technical alternatives. This is in the treatment of salt or waste water. Desalting claims the largest public attention, but methods of advanced waste treatment probably carry the greatest immediate significance. Desalting research has been a runaway panacea promoted by enthusiastic and scientific medicine men in the water management field over the last fourteen years. Desalting is as old as evaporation pans, and major processes for desalting have been in scientific literature for several decades. It was brought into sharp focus by international conferences on arid land and water problems and beginning in 1952 enjoyed a sudden, almost hysterical endorsement by administrators and scientists in the United States.[16] The earlier statements in scientific symposia in the United States were full of caution to the extent to which costs could be reduced to a point permitting use in agriculture.[17] Lively interest turned beyond agriculture to situations of municipal shortage or to opportunities to treat brackish water.

That enthusiasm and support steadily grew is demonstrated by the following series of public statements by Presidents commenting, apparently with the support of their scientific advisers, on the possibilities and need for desalting of sea water:[18]

Harry S Truman—January 10, 1950

Experience in recent years has shown that it may not be possible to meet the shortages of water, which are a threat in some areas, through our extensive water resources programs. I recommend, therefore, that the Congress enact legislation authorizing the initiation of research to find means for transforming salt water into fresh water in large volume at economical costs.

Dwight D. Eisenhower—August 14, 1958

I would hope that high on the agenda of this institution (the United Nations) would be an action to meet one of the major challenges of the Near East, the great common shortage—water.

Much scientific and engineering work is already underway in the field of water development. For instance, atomic isotopes now permit us to chart the courses of great underground rivers. The new horizons are opening in the desalting of water. The ancient problem of water is on the threshold of solution. Energy, determination, and science will carry it over that threshold.

John F. Kennedy—May 25, 1962

When we think of such a large percentage of the world's land which supports so few people, how extraordinary an accomplishment it will be when we can bring water to bear on the deserts surrounding the Mediterranean and the Indian Sea and all the rest. And I think that this is within our grasp and within our lifetime, perhaps even within our decade, and I think it will be the prime accomplishment of science in improving the life of people in the long history of the world. And that is within, as I have said, our reach, and that deserves the greatest effort by us all.

Lyndon B. Johnson—March 30, 1965

The President said enactment of the legislation he proposed "is vital if the Department of the Interior is to mount and lead the substantial sustained effort necessary to achieve truly economic desalting of sea and brackish waters."

Today, a sober assessment of these prospects reveals that extraordinary advances have been made in the technology of desalting by earnest and capable scientists, but that by the cheapest techniques presently in existence it still would be available at a cost which would render it largely useless in most agricultural areas and of limited use in many urban areas. The lowest costs currently anticipated are 15–30 cents per thousand gallons if desalting were to be linked with very large nuclear energy plants on the order of 5,000 megawatts in locations where briny water were readily available.

It should be remembered that these costs are for the production of water and not for its transmission and distribution. In a city such as Chicago water is produced, transported, and distributed for a cost of about 22 cents per thousand gallons. Over the irrigation area of the United States the price paid for water runs from 1 to 7 cents per thousand gallons as a maximum, and it is not unusual for distribution costs to amount to as much as 5 or 10 cents per thousand gallons. Thus, the figure of production cost is only part of the cost and a part which puts desalting very high relative to available water in most parts of the country. Much greater returns from irrigation water than now are reaped would be required to warrant extensive agricultural use of desalted water. To be sure, there are urban areas in deserts or places where briny water would be available for irrigation with a small reduction in salt content where desalting already is a distinct economic alternative just as it is the common source on board oceanliners. To suggest, however, that it may soon bring major change in availability of water and the livelihood of people in other parts of the world, and especially in low-income areas, is to distort the facts grossly.

Under energetic leadership from the Department of the Interior, its Office of Saline Water built up a program of contract research and technical development that progressively reduced the costs of desalting, brought new techniques into operating practice, and demonstrated them in pilot plants.[19] By 1966, about one-fifth of all federal funds for water resources research, as estimated by the Water Resources Research Committee of the Federal Council for Science and Technology, were going into that program.[20] The reasons for such a concentration are not clear, but one of them may well have been the convenience and attraction of heavy reliance upon new hardware.

During the same period there was a much smaller growth of research on the nature of waste waters and ways of removing contaminants. With municipal and industrial users commonly returning from 90 to 95 percent of all water as effluent (power stations consume less than one percent but raise water temperature), the possibility of reusing waste water is important, and when it is recalled that ocean water carries about 30,000 ppm of minerals in contrast to loads one-tenth that amount in many domestic wastes, reuse is especially interesting as a water source. Research on advanced methods of treatment beyond the ordinary primary and secondary treatment has moved ahead by university and government laboratories with support from the Public Health Service and the Federal Water Pollution Control Administration. New chemical, physical, and biological techniques have been developed, the need to integrate them has been recognized, and practical application has been made by both municipal and industrial plants.[21] Increasingly, water reuse, as noted in Chapter IV, has come to be seen as a practicable alternative to stream dilution. In terms of volume of water treated and of breadth of possible application it currently seems more attractive than desalting of sea water.

Why then has desalting been so attractive in the public eye and in the White House? Why have repeated statements held out great promise for bringing the benefits of desalting to millions of underfed and underprivileged people around the world? Perhaps the idea of making the desert bloom is so satisfying. Perhaps it is the attraction of the simple "quick fix" solution in which the scientists and technologists step forward to solve a perplexing human problem with one skillful turn of the laboratory monkey wrench. Perhaps it is because once an administration commitment has been made few people have the courage to stand up and criticize it as being unsuited to the economic and scientific facts of the world. Whatever the explanations, the desalting episode, an episode which is far from closed, is an example of the way in which belief in a single scientific advance may run away with those who espouse it, and it thereby is a warning to those who would expand conscious use of research as a tool of water management. In the desalting experience is a sobering caution for those who would engage in environmental modification on the grand scale, a caution against promising too much too soon, becoming bemused with one answer, against making a public commitment for which there then becomes a political necessity to build support by continuing heavy investment in research which does not fulfill the high hopes.

There is no valid reason for objecting to any research which would extend man's skill in manipulating the environment around him so long as it is coupled with sensitivity to the consequences. And a device for dipping into the great oceanic reservoir of briny water hardly threatens unfavorable repercussions on bordering lands. The current heavy emphasis upon desalting does warrant criticism on other grounds.

The dramatic claims for possible perfection of a means of producing fresh water at a cost of as little as 10 cents per thousand gallons and its use to feed 10 million new mouths each year at a cost of 4 billion dollars in desalting plants diverts attention from basic changes in conditions of water distribution and use which have caused the so-called shortages. Holding out the hope of an early and easy technological remedy encourages some of those who are wasting water to step up their pace in the expectation that help will be forthcoming in the form of plentiful new supplies. It weakens the position of those who would press for revisions in field techniques, pricing schedules, or water rights transfer systems. It discourages consideration of other available alternatives just as the commitment to big dams so long impeded the exploration of other methods.

Fruits of Research

From the first 55 years of watershed experimentation came a deepened understanding of the complexity of interrelations of soil, plants, bedrock, climate, and water in the hydrologic cycle. It piled up weighty caution as to the difficulty of predicting that a change in vegetation in one basin would have the same effect upon runoff in one period as in another period, let alone predicting that the effects would be similar in an adjacent basin. New instrumentation developed, as in the case of lysimeter design and the streamlined spacing of precipitation gauges. Fresh respect was gained for certain of the elementary processes, particularly the role of flow through unsaturated soil in accounting for stream flow. The basis was laid for computer description of drainage basin characteristics. But, with a few exceptions, the major advances came from university groups outside the federal programs. Research on sectors of the hydrologic cycle not directly involved in conventional forest or soil erosion management was not stressed, although creative attention recently has turned to manipulation of snow.

The first 16 years of weather modification research enlarged human understanding of atmospheric processes, particularly convection and the mechanism of nucleation. Techniques for augmenting orographic rainfall, dispersing super-cooled fog, and reducing hail formation were developed. Probing of the mysteries of the atmosphere for these purposes as well as for weather prediction led to the design of models of global circulation patterns holding out the promise of identifying critical points at which massive changes might be stimulated. Although cloud seeding early claimed dominant attention, the research programs of the National Science Foundation and other federal agencies suggest other aspects which may well be more significant in the future. The National Science Foundation and Weather Bureau efforts also confronted, after 7 years delay, the question of how to estimate the full human impacts of altering a parameter of weather. It may be significant that this first conscious federal venture in using research to systematically explore ways of managing a sector of the natural environment was soon accompanied by serious attempts to trace out the possible consequences for ecosystems, hydrologic systems, and systems of human production and communication. A task force on research related to human dimensions of weather modification was set up by the National Center for Atmospheric Research.

Fourteen years of federal study of saline water conversion brought a progressive reduction in the cost of removing minerals from ocean and brackish water. A variety of techniques were explored and improved, and several were demonstrated in pilot plants. Although the emphasis was largely upon what some less respectful observers call plumbing, support was given to basic investigation of the nature of water and of materials it carries in solution. Little attention was given to the conditions in which desalted water might be used at prospective costs. Perhaps the most significant action was the collaboration with scientists of nuclear energy installations in the design of giant nuclear reactors which would reduce the desalting costs by using waste heat from electric power generation.

In only one of the three efforts did social and behavioral research play a major part. The emphasis was on biological and physical relations and on new technology.

With few exceptions public programs for water research have multiple purposes, reflecting no doubt a propensity of federal agencies to look for diverse support. Weather modification and desalting studies claimed possible benefits for farmers, industrialists, and city dwellers, and even the vegetation-runoff studies found utility in providing hydrologic guides for design of small engineering works when their value for land treatment waned. Privately supported research and development has tended to expand the range of means for single purposes, as with improvements in household water supply and waste disposal, independent irrigation, and industrial waste treatment.

Lessons for an Expanding Program

As the United States faces increasingly complex water problems and as it carries out a new cooperative research program, a few observations can be drawn from its experience with these and other ventures in water research.

First, if research on basic relationships is to be more than a bland and stumbling confirmation of the convictions of water and land planners it needs to be carried out in an organization detached from field operations. Attachment to daily management problems and the perpetuation of an agency mission is often incompatible with exploration of new relationships. The opposite may be true of development of technology. In any event, operating agencies should have research units which refine methods and evaluate results.

Second, if radically new techniques are to be devised and tested without strong pressure to prove one the best and with openness to other possible means they should be developed by agencies already having satisfactory operating programs sheltered from fear of criticism of the failures. A Forest Service or a Bureau of Reclamation can take the risk of falling down in a long technological leap so long as its more conventional activities are respected. A Saline Water Office feels under heavy pressure to give the appearance of success, for all seems to depend upon practical results.

Third, so far as research is used consciously as a tool to examine new relationships and new technologies it is likely to take account of their human consequences and thereby suggest still other directions. Studies intended to prove a forest-runoff equation or to perfect a canal lining or a flash evaporation plant for stated needs lead less often to inquiry as to the purpose of water management or the possibility that if other social aims were envisioned different technologies of water management would merit investigation. A new vision of the role of research will inspire new and creative investigations.

Fourth, the properly intriguing possibility that a quick technological fix may for a time solve a pressing social problem may divert attention from either social solutions or other lines of physical and biological research. The desalting drive should be seen as one of a number of tools which contribute to solution, and should not be allowed to obscure attention to the possibility that urgent needs would be reduced by changes in pricing schedules and public attitudes, or to overshadow the study of water reuse or of the great, widely available reservoir of underground water. The social solutions may be exceedingly difficult to execute, and the underlying research may be highly demanding.

One final note—it may be that weather modification demonstrates the importance of thorough canvass of new technological and scientific horizons with the scientific professions before a deep public commitment rather than after. The desalting and weather modification histories stand in contrast. In the case of desalting the government made heavy commitments and then asked for contractors and for conferences to discuss what to do. In the case of weather modification the progress was slower. Researchers were invited to make suggestions, and explorations were started before heavy administrative commitment was made to the programs. One has moved much less dramatically than the other but perhaps with more significant scientific findings and with less chance of unfulfilled claims.

If research were accepted as a major water management tool along with dams, treatment plants, and pricing schedules, the character of water management would be bound to change in several basic ways. Time horizons would be shortened to take account of probable technological change. Measures having lower capital costs and higher operation costs over the shorter periods would be favored. Greater emphasis would be placed on plans preserving flexibility to adjust to new techniques and social instruments as well as to shifting preferences. The range of practicable means would expand and with it the administrative complexity of manipulating the water resource for multiple aims.

To date, the concern of water management with research as a tool has been limited and generally modest, but the prospect is for rapid and solid expansion. The intellectual commitment of university centers to water studies is strong. The new Office of Water Resources Research has supported state water research centers and has begun to stimulate imaginative assessment of research needs.[22] In time it could become the most influential of government agencies dealing with water problems for it has the largest opportunity to operate without being tied to an administrative program or an obligation to show early results.

Moreover, the United States is embarking upon another momentous round of water studies comparable to the "308" reports of the 1920's and 1930's and the drainage basin studies of the 1940's and 1950's. The entire North Atlantic region is covered in one framework study, the Columbia Basin by another, and a third takes shape in the Great Lakes. Opportunities in the framework studies to introduce new methods are large. In the light of the experience with research is it practicable to incorporate in these a formal provision for scientific advance and new technology? Can framework studies be made in a setting in which multiple means, including research, will be canvassed along with multiple purposes before the next great array of dams, treatment plants, and waterways is thrown across the face of our land? Those questions are examined in the concluding chapter.

VI

The five major strategies of water management show signs of coalescing into a sixth and much more complex strategy, embracing features of each and thus far defying precise description. Vaguely defined, this transformation is in the direction of regional integration. Within the framework of either metropolitan areas or groups of drainage basins the public agencies are groping toward an illusive style of planning which would continually explore multiple means of reaching multiple goals. One way of stating the trend and the prospect is to say that the traditional analysis of regional opportunities in terms of linear projec tions of demand leading to long-range plans of public agencies to regulate a finite water supply is moving toward appraisal of a wider range of alternatives, including scientific research, and that the outcome is not a single 50 or 100-year plan but a set of guidelines within which short-term projects by both public and private agencies may be undertaken. While meeting certain of the objections to multiple-purpose public construction, a serious effort at regional integration invites confusion as to administration by drawing in private managers and a large number of local governments and relies more upon public education than upon neat administrative organization to provide continuity and aim.

Linear projection of demand against a finite resource symbolizes a main theme of American water management as it has unfolded in single and multiple-purpose construction programs. To depart from that approach is to invite complexity of analysis, more flexible plans, more systematic use of scientific research, and greater diversity and looseness in administration.

Single-purpose construction by private managers tended to move to either public single-purpose construction or public multiple-purpose construction (Figure VI–1). Navigation, irrigation, and flood control followed the path of single to multiple-purpose construction; hydroelectric power, while predominantly single-purpose private, moved directly to public

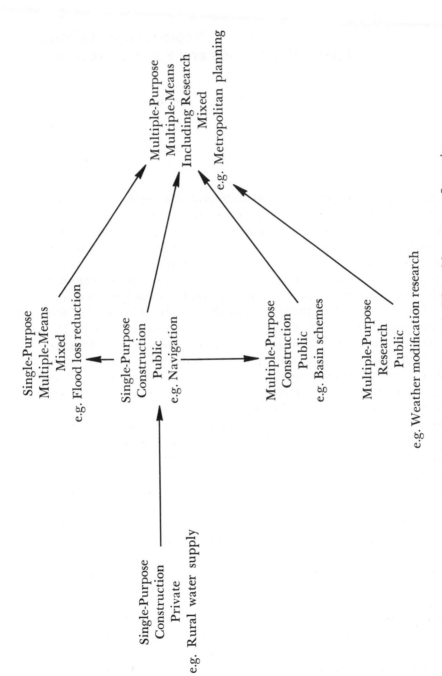

Single-Purpose
Multiple-Means
Mixed
e.g. Flood loss reduction

Single-Purpose
Construction
Public
e.g. Navigation

Multiple-Purpose
Multiple-Means
Including Research
Mixed
e.g. Metropolitan planning

Multiple-Purpose
Construction
Public
e.g. Basin schemes

Multiple-Purpose
Research
Public
e.g. Weather modification research

Single-Purpose
Construction
Private
e.g. Rural water supply

Fig. VI-1—Schematic Diagram of Changes in Water Management Strategies.

multiple-purpose construction. Municipal water supply and waste disposal are edging in the same direction while showing an interesting diversion toward canvassing multiple means. A few of the changes were in the opposite direction, as with a reversal of irrigation development toward single-purpose private construction. The shift to single-purpose multiple-means in the case of flood loss reduction inevitably brought a mixture of public and private activity. The effect of applying public research to water management was largely to refine particular techniques to serve multiple purposes. However, both the strategy of multiple means and of multiple-purpose research when added to multiple-purpose construction so expand the character of drainage basin planning as to suggest that it will be basically different.

A Substitute for Multiple-Purpose Construction?

While there is no clear outline of what this new strategy may be as it looms among gigantic basin plans, a few of its characteristics emerge from the theoretical relation of the several strategies and from planning that is under way. Forms it is denying may be easier to discern than forms it is achieving.

Because of the growing concern for exploration of alternative means and for continuing assessment of the nature of public preferences, the fashioning of a discreet, long-term plan for a basin is fading in prominence. Like the once-popular master plan for urban growth, the comprehensive plan for river basin development loses allegiance among its practitioners. It should do so if for no other reason than the rapidly changing technical suitability of engineering works by comparison with the long time horizons required for their economic justification. To speak of a system of storage reservoirs on the Potomac River costing at least $160,000,000 as justified by benefits of low water regulation flowing over 50 years when the pace of improvement in waste treatment and the spatial pattern of urban living promises radical changes in 20 years is to run the risk of built-in obsolescence.

There also seems little doubt that while the complexity of problems canvassed calls for a stronger coordinating role by one agency—the Corps of Engineers, the Bureau of Reclamation, or a new drainage basin commission—it also prohibits vesting full public responsibility for planning in any such entity. The diversity of interests drawn together in water planning for any one area precludes their being served adequately by the operations of one agency, particularly as the range of devices considered by public agencies is widened. As means of coping with

water problems multiply, the idea of finding a solution by a single construction program seems less and less suitable.

It is especially cumbersome to translate a program relying on construction plans and water allocations into an interstate compact which
will satisfy national goals and regional equities, or to settle interstate
allocations by going to court. The Great Lakes Diversion case is an
example of a tragic waste of public funds and time centered on a single
engineering solution. Instead of building up elaborate evidence for or
against a relatively small diversion of Lake Michigan water to supplement Illinois River flow asserting a local proprietary control of the
nation's water, the cities and states of the basin could have joined in
exploring the full range of possible ways of handling waste and regulating water quality in the Lakes system. (An abortive attempt was made
to bring the four Lake Michigan states together in 1929.) Ultimately,
they will be obliged to do this cooperatively.[1] Meanwhile, the wisest
judicial decision is a poor substitute for joint appraisal of the technical,
economic, and administrative alternatives open to them.

Another way of describing the type of strategy which might replace
multiple-purpose construction is to outline trends in aspects of the decision process. Aims have become progressively more numerous and
ambiguous. When means have multiplied they have sharpened the recognition of aims, and have tended to develop around limited purposes.
During the expansion of multiple-purpose public construction the time
horizons lengthened, but with more consideration of alternative means
and of scientific research as one of those means, the horizons have begun
to shorten. From a situation in which heavy risks were taken in private
resource management, there has been a gradual reduction in hazards of
shortage and excess, accompanied in recent years by doubts as to the
degree that reliance should be placed upon engineering measures in
contrast with other methods of spreading risk. The spatial extent of
planning has spread from local navigation and irrigation projects to
stream reaches, entire basins and then groups of basins, but with attention to economic analysis and to multiple means the scope has enlarged
on the one hand to consideration of genuinely national efficiency and
has contracted on the other hand to assessment of the complex of possible measures within metropolitan areas. Concern for recognition and
measurement of environmental impacts has increased at an accelerating pace. The long-term trend toward heavier public investment has
been modified modestly by increasing attention to specialized and
dispersed management, such as nuclear power and household waste
disposal.

A strategy which meets the principal objections to multiple-purpose public construction in a theoretically viable fashion would have the following characteristics. Its aims would be multiple and consciously recognized as evolving with public preferences which in themselves would be partly shaped by the process followed. Its means would be multiple, and would take account of a full range of alternatives, including scientific research as a tool for devising new technologies affecting both demand and supply. For that reason, it would utilize a mixture of public and private administrative instruments, encouraging as much decentralization of choice among individuals and local agencies as consistent with broad guidelines supported by public consensus. Standards for water quality, hazard reduction, and social valuation would not be rigid, but decisions would be based on criteria of keeping the range of choice as wide as practicable and of working toward short-time horizons within frameworks describing long-term human needs and physical limits. There would be intensive investigation of resources and the theoretical possibilities and social consequences of altering them. Because the populations served are likely to be in dispersed metropolitan areas and because the locus of political decision will rest there, the planning would need to take account of metropolitan organization. It would be alert to the distinctive hydrologic unity of drainage basins and aquifers, but would not attempt to conform the social process of choice to the physical entities of watershed lines. Whether or not such a strategy may be achieved is conjectural. However, several trends support it.

With the spread of sprinkler irrigation, the diversification of flood loss reduction measures, the increasing independence of residential and industrial water installations, the creation of drainage basin commissions such as the Delaware, the launching of special surveys such as the Northeast Water Supply Survey, and the prominence of cities in regional water controversies, as in the Great Lakes, the direct role of individual and local managers in water planning is more explicit. The part played by the Los Angeles metropolitan area in exploring opportunities for linking desalting with nuclear reactors is symptomatic of growing organization of water management in the expanding structure of metropolitan areas. While a few years ago the negotiation of interstate arrangements for water was thought of primarily as a state responsibility, the reapportionment of legislative votes among urban and rural constituencies, the strength of urban planning agencies, and the declining relative importance of agriculture have raised the importance of the city clusters in dealing with other states as well as with federal agencies.

Indicative of a radical departure from the tradition of authorizing specific water projects to meet vaguely stated needs was the Appalachian program of 1965. Water development was treated as only one of several activities, including highway and education development, which might serve a broad aim of income redistribution in assisting a chronically depressed area.[2] Not only did the customary goal of economic efficiency as measured by national productivity give way to redistribution aims similar to the authorization of special irrigation projects in drought-stricken areas during the late 1930's, but the evaluation of projects was seen as comparing water with other types of investment.

Projections of Municipal Water Needs

The most elementary feature of water planning throughout the United States and many other parts of the world is the linear projection embodied in the municipal water supply engineer's curve of water use in a growing city and its extrapolation into the future either geometrically or according to some relation to anticipated change in population or economic activity. Whether a simple extension of the curve, oftentimes a straight line, or related to social factors, the demand projection is used assiduously in such activities as the Bureau of Reclamation forecast of national food needs, the drainage basin study's forecast of power and recreation needs, and the Senate Select Committee's estimate of needs for dilution of stream flow to the year 2000.

Projection methods are illustrated from practices in nine large cities in the United States (see Table VI–1). All begin with statistics as to water pumpage and population over the period of record. Usually where the data permit they are compiled for smaller divisions of the city and its outlying consuming areas. If there are separate records on industrial uses these are handled separately, as at Houston, but commonly the various uses cannot be distinguished beyond rough estimates of the proportion which each contributes to total usage. Past pumpage is divided by estimated population to obtain per capita use. Beyond this point the method of analysis and projection follow somewhat different paths in reaching a probable volume requirement for a target year.

The simplest procedure is to extend the volume of pumpage as a straight line or in a curvilinear fashion for the desired period. A common refinement is to relate total water use to the population served, and to then project future use on the basis of estimates by demographers as to what future population will be and by administrators as to what areas will be served by the system. When per capita usage enters into projections it may be applied by assuming present rates of use will continue, by simply extrapolating the past rate of change in per capita use, or by estimating the factors which might affect use. As shown at Chicago and New York, it may be misleading to assume per capita use will continue to climb.

Attempts to adjust for changes in conditions affecting per capita use may draw on a variety of analyses. One of the obvious engineering questions is whether or not there will be significant changes in leakage as a result of improvements, extensions, and pumping pressure; reductions of per capita use in the Chicago suburbs from 140 in 1960 to 133 in 1965 in contrast with projected values of 158 and 165 respectively probably were due in part to curbing of leakage and wastage. An economic question is whether there will be changes in the quality and mix of economic activity which would change use significantly. Thus, the Washington projections anticipate increases in level of living that would raise water use, and Los Angeles estimates that a growing proportion of multiunit dwellings will reduce use sufficiently to offset increases in per capita use elsewhere, keeping the same unit figure. A marked change in the type of industrial use would be significant but rarely is the subject of prediction (Houston made a special study of this factor).

The operators and consulting engineers properly are inclined to take an optimistic view of conditions making for growth in use, for if they overestimate, the costs will be covered by operating and capital charges but if they underestimate they may be blamed for temporary inconvenience of the citizenry or for holding back vital civic progress. Their projections must also cover maximum daily and hourly requirements which place more severe constraints on system design. The result finally is one curve or high and low curves for future needs, as illustrated by Figure VI-2 for Detroit. That the actual may come close to the prediction also is illustrated by Detroit's study of 1924 (Figure VI-3): more often it falls short, as at Philadelphia and Chicago.

Insofar as the projection methods promote overinvestment in water supply they are inefficient, and Hirshleifer, de Haven and Milliman have shown the pitfalls.[3] Quite aside from other considerations of planning there would be national benefit in curbing inoptimal investment. To a major degree the projection of requirements can only be as accurate as the demographic projections which are made by others; and by the time an unsuitable population forecast has been applied with conservative allowance for changes in service areas, wastage, and per capita use, the difference between projection and performance may become very large.

This is a straightforward and rather satisfactory way of going about estimating needs for providing additional supplies. Why alter it? It has

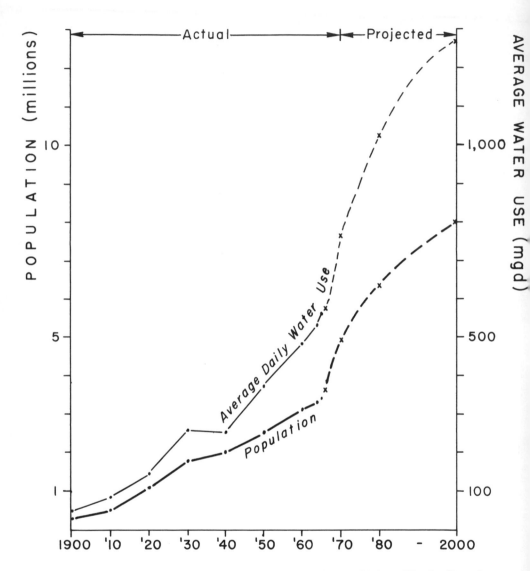

Fig. VI-2—Actually and Projected Population and Water Use for Detroit
Metropolitan Area, 1900–2000. Per capita use is expected to increase more
rapidly than population.

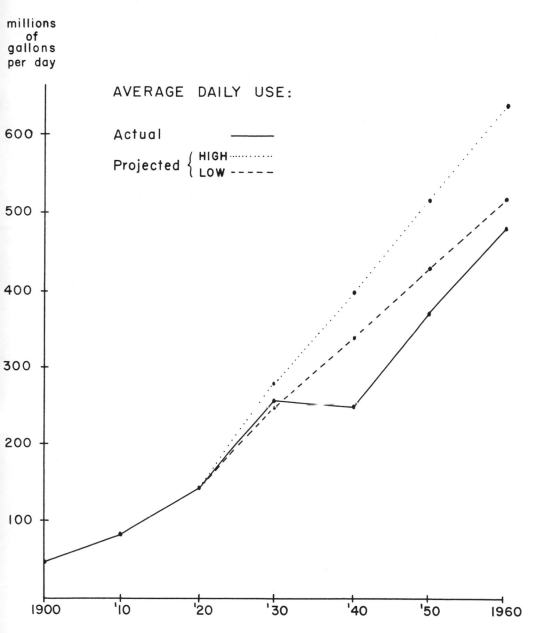

Fig. VI–3—Actual Water Use and 1924 Projection for Detroit Metropolitan Area, 1900–1960. Although the projection proved high for the decade of the 1930's, it did describe the general trend in subsequent decades.

worked relatively well up to the present. Overdesign has been more attractive to city fathers in large population centers than underdesign. Only when a city such as New York has been slow in taking steps to provide supplies which it knew it would require have there been difficult shortages. Here and there shortages have existed for a longer period of time but by and large the municipalities of the United States have managed to get as much water as they wanted when they wanted it.

The basic deficiency of this form of analysis is not that it has failed to forecast needs to date but that it fosters an approach to water management which carries other, heavier disabilities. By concentrating on projection of past trends, attention is drawn away from other variables in the situation. There is strong inclination to ignore further improvements which would reduce leakage, or education and inspection programs aimed at cutting wastage. Changes in pricing schedules and metering may be omitted from consideration, and although the residential use of water is believed to be relatively price inelastic, price may have an influence on consumption. Opportunities to revise the water-using equipment over time through building regulations may be neglected.

A fundamental difficulty is that the water resource is finite and that this kind of projection cannot go on indefinitely. Sooner or later a stage will come when the projections of linear growth will exceed the amount of water which then is available. A common answer is that when that time arrives, a time that is comfortably distant for many areas, necessary steps will be taken either to reduce use or to find substitute water sources. However, even if the supply were infinite, which it is not, there might be wiser solutions in terms of the amount and character of investment required. Opportunities to make use of waters of different quality for different purposes, as in disposing of waste water, or to capture rainfall in urban areas or to recharge otherwise depleted aquifers from flood flows await investigation. Substitutes for water as a transporter of material and heat in industrial processes offer attractive possibilities. The Malthusian trap of believing that demand is bound to rise till misery sets in and that resources cannot be utilized beyond present capacity can be avoided.

Background of Metropolitan Planning in Northeastern Illinois

Is it sanguine to look to any combination of private and public managers so managing the water resource in an urbanized society as to deal with multiple aims by multiple means, including scientific research and having flexibility as a major criterion? The northeastern Illinois study is reviewed in part because it set out with high hopes of reaching a port of integrated yet flexible planning, and in part because it ran onto rocks of analysis and interpretation which threaten the course of any such regional voyage.

Far less detailed than the "type 1" framework study now blanketing the country, it may nevertheless exemplify a variation in procedure which if widely accepted would profoundly affect future strategy. The lively interest displayed by Southern California agencies in desalting and sewage reuse, the broad examination of technological opportunities sponsored by the Regional Plan Association of New York, the attempt at unified study of Hudson River land and water, and the controversy over possible alternatives in coping with waste and flood problems in the Lower Potomac suggest an openness to the approach which the northeastern Illinois study represents.

A great number of groups are concerned with finding sound solutions to problems of water shortage and water surplus in the northeastern Illinois metropolitan area.[4] At the municipal level 250 water departments, 120 drainage districts, and 43 sanitary districts operate (see Figure VI-4). Four of the six counties exercise control over new waste installations through health departments, three have planning commissions, five forest preserve districts, and two public works departments. State authorities include the State Water Survey, the Geological Survey, the Division of Waterways, the Division of Fisheries, the Division of Soil and Water Conservation, and the Division of Water Resources, all but two of them under different departmental guidance. At the federal level, the Corps of Engineers, Water Pollution Control Administration, Geological Survey, Soil Conservation Service, Weather Bureau, and Housing Agency carry programs of study and operations. In addition, the Metropolitan Sanitary District, centering on Cook County, manages large waste disposal works and exercises enforcement powers on water quality. The Northeastern Illinois Planning Commission enjoys modest advisory and coordinating powers from the state but has no large continuing study functions such as the federal investigations of Great Lakes water quality under the WPCA or of Upper Mississippi water development under the Corps of Engineers, and the counties and municipalities are jealous of their planning powers.

The northeastern Illinois effort to take a fresh view of water resources needs had its root in two situations. One was the Salt Creek skirmishes. These were a series of encounters among local, state, and federal agencies during 1958–60 over flood water disposal in the Chicago

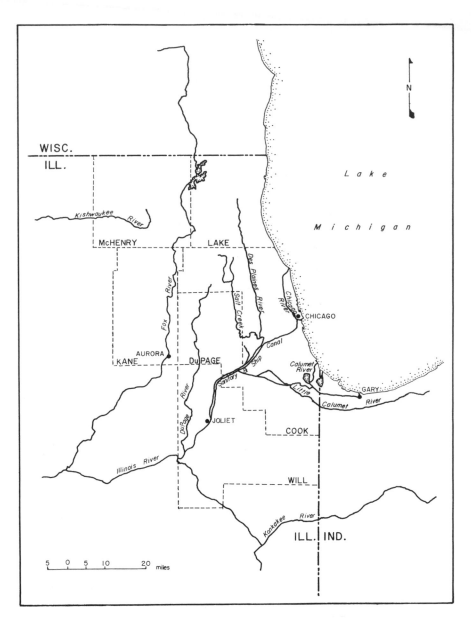

Fig. VI-4—Sketch Map of Northeastern Illinois Metropolitan Area.

metropolitan area.[5] The most prominent was that over Salt Creek in which the state Division of Waterways proposed to channelize the stream at state expense to provide protection from floods for people along the banks and, far more important, to sufficiently reduce the flow line in high water periods so that sewerage systems in adjoining municipalities could construct sewer discharge by gravity with a minimum of lift. The aim of the municipalities was to reduce pumping cost and the expense of principal interceptor sewer lines. The lower channel above the junction with the Des Plaines River would be cut through a Cook County forest preserve. Forest preserve officials properly asked whether this was an effective way of meeting the needs of adjoining property owners and whether it was a suitable way of handling the natural environment of the flood plain. Out of the controversy came discussions among interested agencies and citizens who had been brought together by the Northeastern Illinois Planning Commission to look into broader issues. Their review led to enunciation of a general policy for dealing with disposal of flood waters in the area and the initiation of what was to become, in cooperation with the U.S. Geological Survey, the first comprehensive mapping of flood hazard in any metropolitan area.[6] The episode revealed common interests in water management, established a mechanism for cooperative study, and showed possible gains from tying in water supply activities with flood water control.

Shortly thereafter the Commission instituted a review of water supply problems. These had been much in public thinking because lake states other than Illinois had challenged the continued and proposed increased diversion of water from Lake Michigan for water supply and dilution of waste in the Illinois River by Illinois and the City of Chicago. A proposal by three suburban towns to go directly to the lake for domestic water was held up. The city of Chicago and the state submitted evidence to a special master appointed by the U.S. Supreme Court to the effect that water needs of the area would continue to grow and that it would be increasingly necessary for the city to draw on the lake. This was a case of linear projection. The justification for such a projection as given by the State Water Survey was as follows:[7]

> . . . on the basis of presently available information additional Lake Michigan water will be needed in the Chicago metropolitan area. Elmhurst, Villa Park, and Lombard, because of the failing present sources, because of the lack of reasonable alternatives, and because of high pumping rates, are in the area of most critical need for change to the Lake water.

Metropolitan Review of Alternatives

Against this background the Commission moved ahead in 1962 with a comprehensive study of alternatives, using an urban planning grant from the Housing and Home Finance Agency. It was comprehensive insofar as northeastern Illinois was concerned but political restrictions unfortunately excluded adjoining parts of Wisconsin and Indiana from its review of both needs and supplies. It examined a wide range of ways in which water use might be changed while population and manufacturing activity increased.[8]

The extent to which industries in the area were currently using established water conservation devices was examined along with factors explaining differences in adoption of new techniques. Among the alternatives considered for residential water use was that of finding substitute sources of water from waste water disposal for lawn watering. Estimates were made of what water use would be if leakage were reduced to a reasonable level in each of the municipalities involved. Attention was given to the possibility of designing flood control channel improvements so as to promote the recharge of shallow aquifers. Studies were made of the possibility of using large underground reserves over temporary periods of shortage and thus occasionally mining the ground water to take care of emergency conditions which otherwise would require heavy investment in rarely used surface water storage. Combinations of flood plain valley storage and floodproofing were investigated. A special examination of links between urban land use and water management by the U.S. Geological Survey was initiated. Opportunities to join stream improvement with urban renewal and wildlife preservation were explored. Examples of comprehensive management schemes for small areas, including sample industrial installations, were presented.

The result was not a single projection of future water use which could be compared with available supply but a series of projections based on different assumptions as to the degree to which technology would be employed by different sectors of the population and a series of appraisals of potentially interesting methods of changing supply. For each county, as shown in aggregate in Figure VI–5, uses were projected by: (1) extrapolating past trends in per capita use (a modification of the evidence presented by Illinois agencies in the lake diversion case); (2) continuing present per capita use on the assumption that reductions through plumbing improvement, industrial reuse, leak detection, and air conditioning would offset increases from other causes; and (3) assuming known conservation techniques would be generally adopted. In

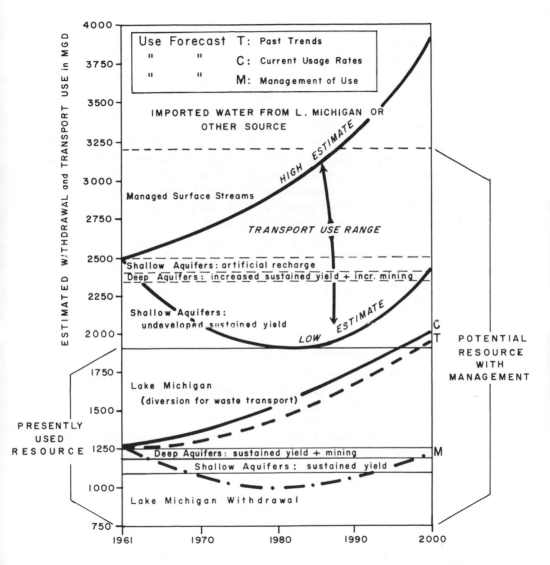

Fig. VI–5—Water Use and Supply Projections for the Northeastern Illinois Metropolitan Area, 1961–2000. The high and low estimates of supply reflect different assumptions as to technology, regulations, and other factors.

addition, the volume of water required to dilute resulting effluents was estimated on a range between present use and improved management.

Consideration was given to the possibility that technology itself might change in a predictable fashion. A variety of experts were consulted, and encouragement to think that powerful advances were in prospect was received, but none of the judgments seemed sufficiently strong to warrant a fourth type of projection.

Each set of projections was compared on a county basis with estimates of water supply under different management conditions. It was specified that the accessible resource would depend upon choice of technology, social regulation, and criteria of investment and risk bearing. The report did not present a single plan for water development. Rather, it offered a broad strategy in which the principal criteria for selection of projects would reject the fragmented "straight-line" strategy which had governed Chicago's water management. According to the report, that consisted primarily of withdrawing water from Lake Michigan. To achieve an effective separation of drinking water and waste water, the used water is discharged into a canal system that flows into the Illinois River and which provides a navigation link between Lake Michigan and the Mississippi River. The principles governing an expanded strategy were seen as including:

1. Beginning with a definition of the goals of metropolitan development, such as alternative patterns of urban land use.

2. Identifying the practical range of management measures available for use in given circumstances.

3. Maintaining maximum flexibility in decision making as to available measures in order to avoid total commitment to any one solution.

4. Pressing for rigorous social evaluation of proposed measures.

5. Bringing land planning into water management in dealing with maintenance of recreational waters, the effect of urban construction on infiltration rates, reservation of flood plains for suitable uses, and location of waste disposal.

6. Coordinating the effects of upstream and downstream measures on both an interstate and intercounty basis.

While it was thought desirable to use scientific research as a tool in devising new solutions, the funds did not permit such activity.

Heavy emphasis was placed upon keeping as many alternatives open in the future as possible, and upon being alert to the opportunities to adopt new technologies as they become available. Discussions in preparing the report led to exploration of certain kinds of techniques which had not previously been considered. One example was the possible construction of tunnels deep in the limestone between the adjoining river systems and Lake Michigan to permit storage of flood waters underground or in the lake with a view to later withdrawal in dry periods and with incidental benefits for hydroelectric power generation. Another advance in technique was in assessment of favorable grounds for shallow aquifer recharge.

The report issued in August 1966 became the subject of lively discussion in the metropolitan area as well as in other areas where the linear projection had been the conventional mode of approach. That the response has been mixed is illustrative of growing differences in view between state and urban governments in other areas. Within the metropolitan area, the adoption of the deep-tunnel idea by the City of Chicago and the Metropolitan Sanitary District was prompt and momentous. Several municipalities (Arlington Heights and Hinsdale), which had been looking to purchase of Lake Michigan water to meet rising demand, turned to wells. Greater interest was shown in shallow aquifers as potential sources. Park Forest acquired a natural recharge area as a green belt along Thorn Creek. Recharge potential was made a criterion for land purchase in DuPage County's expansion program. A number of communities, such as Joliet, undertook leakage surveys and waste control programs. Attention to ordinances managing water use grew in several municipalities. The concept of flood water storage as claiming space wherever compatible with other uses led to new designs for parking lots, roofs, and building complexes in at least seven towns. Two of the exemplary local projects for unified water management were moved toward construction. Flood plain regulations became commonplace. The interest of industry in new schemes for water collection, storage, and reuse heightened. Over a two-year period, the positive response was in this sense heartening, but from the adverse reactions perhaps some lessons can be learned that are more generally applicable to water resources management.

Conflicts with Conventional Programs

Although several of the state agencies participated in the study, shared funds, and joined in the drafting of the final report, the governor objected to its release in final form as written by the staff of the Commission with the advice of a technical advisory committee. Critics argued that it would be irresponsible for the Commission to issue a report recommending consideration of the river-lake tunnel scheme or occasional mining of ground water. The first seemed likely to confuse a public which had already been told there was one simple solution in the form of drawing water from the lake. The second was regarded as contrary to "sound conservation principles." In addition, it was believed that release of a report suggesting alternatives to the state's testimony in the Great Lakes diversion case as to the amount of water which the area would require in the future might jeopardize the position of the state, and impair the welfare of the city. Moreover, it was considered unsuitable to burden the public with weighing a variety of possible solutions. In sum, consideration of alternatives would rock the political boat, challenge some professional views, stir up the public to think in unconventional and difficult ways, and jeopardize the state's claimed vested right in the waters of Lake Michigan.

To openly canvass a range of unconventional solutions exposes the investigator to the professional caution of individuals and the protective opposition of agencies committed to the conventional. It is difficult for agencies engaged in construction programs to stand back and question the validity of the very programs to which their names are attached. This kind of question was raised by the Metropolitan Sanitary District when the idea of river-lake tunnels first was proposed and it was interesting that although the idea severely challenged the main surface water distribution works which the District had been constructing and for which it had enlarged plans for the future, it picked up the new idea and devoted some of its funds to a pilot exploration of the other alternatives. Much of the outcome would seem to depend upon the agency's sense of involvement in the new ideas before they command public debate.

Presenting a Complex Choice

Beyond the question of how many alternatives people can consider in any given situation is that of how much complexity they can comprehend. Some administrators thought it unreasonable to ask a group of citizens or a committee of heads of citizen's organizations to attempt to canvass more than two or three alternatives for dealing with a particular problem. It seemed especially inappropriate to solicit opinions on the values at stake until a definite recommendation had been prepared by the professionals.

In the northeastern Illinois area there were no well-established means of sounding out citizen preferences or of instigating discussion of complex problems. Without such organization, it was extremely awkward for the Commission to reach political groups responsible for making new water investments or regulations. Their technical staffs doubted the wisdom of inviting comment.

Where to Center Administrative Responsibility?

It also became evident that the Commission suffered from having no special sanctions which it would apply against those who opposed its effort to provide an impartial appraisal. Insofar as the operating agencies could learn from the new ideas which were acceptable to them they were ready to do so. Insofar as the new ideas seemed to challenge existing positions they were free to criticize, to place obstructions, and to fail to cooperate. The Commission could do little by way of defense. It could only make plain what it regarded to be the choices open to the citizens of the area. In a sense, this situation is similar to that faced by the Natural Resources Planning Board in the early 1940's when operating federal agencies and the Congress found its existence a discomfort. A planning agency gains continued support in part from legislatively given sanctions but in large measure from confidence and support of agencies and citizen's groups who find it useful because of its daily work.

It is important to find leadership for such an enterprise that is not wholly federal or as wholly permissive and voluntary as most metropolitan planning agencies. The drainage basin commissions being established by the Water Resources Council may offer occasion for a new kind of cooperative study. Coordinating committees of the federal framework investigations will be a step in the same direction if they can involve the vital urban governments in active assessment of water plans.

To the extent that multiple means are appraised the number of responsible public and private managers enlarges. When flood loss reduction is viewed chiefly as building a levee, the Corps of Engineers and the local taxing authority are the only agencies that need settle matters of project design, rights of way, and local contributions. When floodproofing, emergency measures, and insurance of residual damages are seen as desirable means, the execution of program calls for understanding collaboration of property owners, local architects and engineers, municipal planners and engineers, and insurance and financial agencies. As demonstrated in northeastern Illinois, it may be more reasonable from an administrative standpoint for them to be related by understanding of general guidelines and by sharing in use of flood hazard maps than by agreement as to specific plans.[9]

Projecting Science and Technology

It would be difficult as well as needlessly costly for northeastern Illinois or any other great urban area and for the North Atlantic Regional study as well as any other framework investigation to make its own imaginative appraisal of ways in which scientific knowledge might change the art of water management. The Chicago attempt did not succeed in canvassing all major opportunities, although it did spur two important innovations. Nor has there been a national effort to examine the implications of scientific advances for water planning. Ackerman and Löf gave an admirable review of the place of technology as of 1958.[10] But scientists, many of them having no direct interest in water use and control, need to be confronted with the aspirations and daily problems of those who commit themselves and successive generations to gigantic schemes applying current knowledge. Virtually all of the troublesome problems are national or international in incidence, and there is no regional monopoly on either curiosity or competency.

A combination of the Water Resources Council, the Federal Council on Science and Technology, and the National Academy of Sciences-National Research Council-National Academy of Engineering could perform a fruitful service by bringing together natural scientists, social scientists, engineers, and other water managers periodically to canvass the implications of scientific advances and potentials.[11] Out of such an exercise might come to regional groups a set of judgments, avoiding a single forecast, as to technological changes which may be expected on the basis of existing knowledge and as to directions in which research seems to be advancing rapidly. Judgments would be offered as to possible shifts in demand or in practicable tools: new uses, substitutes, techniques.

Two side benefits might accrue. Members of the scientific community not normally involved in water management might become intrigued with certain of the issues: creative responses are more likely to be provoked by arousing individual curiosity than by organized research programs. At the same time the opportunities to strengthen international collaboration in dealing with basic problems might be enhanced. Although there is rather full exchange of scientific findings and techniques through constituent members of the International Council of Scientific Unions and engineering groups like the World Power Conference and the International Congress on Irrigation and Drainage, special attempts at collaboration such as the Arid Zones Research Programme, the International Hydrologic Decade, and the International Biological Programme speed up the process and focus attention on critical relationships in the world of nature. Thus far, there has been little exciting collaboration in attacking uncharted sectors of water management and, particularly, the social sciences as they affect alternatives and the decision process. A systematic national effort at projecting scientific and technologic advances and needs would spur such international exploration.

The Role of Public Information

Understanding of guidelines as to aims and means requires a degree of informed judgment by the officials and interest groups concerned that rarely is present in water planning. That it is possible is shown by the breadth and intensity of debate generated by plans for Colorado River dams or Potomac River cleanup. But as the discussion of hearing procedure in Chapter IV suggests, it is doubtful that adequate flow of information can be sustained without using special educational methods when sharp conflicts of economic and aesthetic judgments are absent, or when crisis does not threaten. Evidence on this point is sparse. Most of the systematic efforts at public education about the choices available in specific areas, such as the masterful work of the Delaware Basin citizens group,[12] and the widespread appraisals of water policy by local chapters of the League of Women Voters,[13] necessarily have been directed at plans drawn by federal or interstate agencies. Such information programs build on but are different from broader education to cultivate understanding of resource management and conservation.

The type of biennial review of water needs and supply anticipated by the Senate Select Committee and authorized as a duty for the Water Resources Council is yet to be tested in the public arena. That national assessment report, recognizing regional differences, bringing together the thinking of the chief agencies and properly presented for public review, might prove a vehicle for carrying facts and modes of approach to citizen groups and local officials at regular intervals. No less important might be the influence of preparing those estimates upon the thinking of the agencies themselves, for if the findings were couched in estimates of need and of prospects for technological change they could bring forward new ideas that tend to be submerged in the pressure to present construction projects and to defend them. The preponderant amount of information pouring out of the operating agencies is in support of their programs as authorized by the Congress, and only a small amount of the essentially factual type, such as that issued by the Geological Survey on water supply, serves broader purposes. Congressional committees dealing with water and land have an obligation to make special efforts to appraise the natural resources situation as thoroughly as their counterpart committees examine the national economic situation, but they lack certain data and analytical methods.

As in the case of assessing consumer preferences, any attempt to promote public discussion as to limits and opportunities for water management would be bound to influence the quality of public opinion on those points. If wise sounding of public attitudes toward environment involves presenting citizens with viable choices and the evidence about them, then it follows that the assessment of preferences should be closely linked with a public information program that presents choices rather than evangelizes for an agency doctrine.

Changes Within Existing Organization

The history of administrative organization for water management in the United States offers little hope that a reorientation of approach would be translated into drastic shifts in government organization. Agency missions and Congressional committee structure at best are slow to change. Yet, the changes which are needed do not seem to require substantial alteration of governmental structure. The Corps of Engineers, the Bureau of Reclamation, the emerging basin commissions, and many municipal, district, and industrial organizations have sufficient authority to carry out a regional integration approach. Moreover, much of the new activity would be by agencies whose principal functions are not concerned with water. Administrative obstacles there are, and legal complications aplenty; none of them seems crippling. What is most lacking is a widely shared sense of strategy, a strategy that recognizes multiple aims, that freely canvasses multiple means, and that places high value on maintaining flexibility. This would seem practicable in the framework studies now unfolding and in the detailed studies which continue. Such a strategy could not be sustained without persistent use of scientific research as a tool and without a sensitive sounding of public preferences linked with public education. It would require keener attention to the complex network of managers who decide how water is used, and to the intricate involvement of water management with aspirations and plans for reshaping the whole quality of environment for a rapidly urbanizing population.

Tasks for a National Water Commission

Two functions on a national scale probably could not be performed by existing agencies, and could be handled by an agency like the proposed national water commission. One is to guide the transitions in policy which will be required as a greater range of means is employed. When questions such as the mix of structural and non-structural measures in flood loss reduction or the integration of desalting with cloud seeding and phreatophyte control measures in the arid basins are raised, it is important to have an agency for weighing the promise of each and for suggesting ways of modifying prevailing federal policies so as to accommodate them.

A second is to deal with the spatial distribution effects of technical, evaluative, and financial policies in water management. Underlying much of the federal and state investment in water projects has been a vague but powerful belief that they would carry special benefits to certain areas—the arid West, or the inland empire, or Appalachia, to name only three. As geographic research gives greater precision to the measurement of those impacts on society and physical environment, and as the areal spread of new projects enlarges, questions of national preference are brought into prominence. If there is water going unused in Oregon should it be transferred to Arizona or should population be attracted to use it in Oregon? What would be the extent of resulting dislocations across the country? Should investment in new water projects be used, if it could be, to encourage maintenance of population in Appalachia or to enhance opportunities for Appalachian migrants in areas to which they are moving? Such issues deserve careful evaluation by a group other than the operating agencies before going to the Congress for final decision.

These two services could be rendered by a national agency using the experience of, but not directly responsible to, the chief federal and state administrative agencies. From the performance of the Outdoor Recreation Resources Review Commission and the Senate Select Committee in translating their proposals into action, there would be merit in Congressional participation and membership from the outset.

Attitudes Toward Nature

At base, this emerging strategy reflects a shift in man's attitude toward nature and his concomitant role in society. The view of man the transformer or man the conqueror that permeates so much of the single and multiple-purpose construction and that shows itself in the chart of the future as a contest between rising human demands for water and bounded natural supplies is replaced by another. In the view of man as the cooperator, man the harmonizer, construction is only one means of coming to terms with an environment he never fully explores and that is constantly changing under his hand. With the adoption of this view, the means and instruments of handling water become increasingly complex, the concern with tracing environmental impacts more acute, the adjustments to human preferences increasingly sensitive, and the demand for citizen participation heavier. The emphasis shifts from construction to scientific probing, and from long-term commitment to short-term flexibility.

TABLE VI–1

PROJECTIONS OF FUTURE WATER NEEDS—NINE U.S. CITIES

City	Date and Time Horizon of Projection	Per Capita Use In Gallons Daily Current	Projected	Method of Projecting Need*
New York	1966–2010	154	182	Extrapolate use trends for projected population for each borough.
Chicago	1955–80	234	245	Extrapolate use trends for projected domestic and industrial users separately for each community.
Philadelphia	1946–2000	180	180	For population increase of 20%, estimated that increases in air conditioning and suburban use would be offset by increases in industrial and distributional efficiency.
Philadelphia (including Trenton)	1965–2010	115 maximum	169	Extrapolates increased per capita use for projected population and economic activity.
Detroit (6 counties)	1957–2000	242	350	Extrapolates increased per capita use for projected population for separate communities.
	1959–2000	147	164	Extrapolates to 1980 for separate communities on basis of load, and extrapolates for aggregate thereafter.
	1966–2000	157	159	Using population projections from several sources, estimates slight increases in use.
Baltimore	1962–2010	146 (1960)	203	Separate estimates for domestic public, commercial, and industrial users.
Houston	circa 1960–2010	Aggregate only		
Washington	1946–2000	155 (1940)	161	Applies modest increase in per capita use to estimated increase in population.

TABLE VI–1—*Continued*

City	Date and Time Horizon of Projection	Per Capita Use In Gallons Daily Current	Projected	Method of Projecting Need*
Washington (metropolitan area)	1962–2010	160	210	Separate estimates for increased standard of living and for increased industrial activity.
St. Louis	1966–80	259	300	Extrapolate per capita use trends.
Minneapolis-St. Paul	1960–80	aggregate only		Extrapolate per capita use trends for projected population

* The description of projection methods does not give the details of calculations. Attention is directed at any factors other than linear projection of past trends in population and per capita use.

Sources

1. *Report of the Board of Water Supply of the City of New York on the Third City Tunnel, 1st Stage, 1966.*
2. Alvord, Burdick, and Howson, *Report upon Adequate Water Supply for Chicago Metropolitan Area, 1955–1980.*
3. Bureau of Municipal Research of Philadelphia, *Philadelphia's Water Supply, 1946.*
4. U.S., 87th Congress, 2d Session, *Delaware River Basin,* House Document No. 522, 1960.
5. National Sanitation Foundation, *A Report on the Water Supply for the Six County Metropolitan Area, Southeastern Michigan, 1957.*
6. *Detroit's Water Development Program for the Metropolitan Area.* Report to the City of Detroit Board of Water Commissioners, 1959.
7. *Detroit's Water Development Program for Southeastern Michigan, 1966.*
8. A. F. Broyles, "Planning the Future of a Distribution System," *Journal of American Water Works Association* (1966), pp. 526–34.
9. Brown and Root, Inc., *The Long Range Plan of Water Supply for the City of Houston, Texas,* n.d.
10. U.S., 79th Congress, 2d Session, *Adequate Future Water Supply for District of Columbia and Metropolitan Area,* House Document No. 480, 1946.
11. U.S., Army Engineer District, *Potomac River Basin,* 1962, V, Appendix E.
12. Personal communications from W. T. Malloy, Director of Public Utilities, and D. C. Guilfoy, Deputy Water Commissioner, St. Louis.
13. Twin Cities Metropolitan Planning Commission, *Metropolitan Plan Report No. 6, Metropolitan Water Study, Part III,* 1960.

Notes

CHAPTER I

1. These estimates are drawn from U.S. Department of Commerce, *Water Resources Developments, Capital Investment Values, 1900–1977* (June, 1959), extended by using *Construction Statistics* for subsequent years.

2. U.S., President's Water Resources Policy Commission, *A Water Policy for the American People* (Washington: Government Printing Office, 1950), p. 18.

3. U.S., Tennessee Valley Authority, *Nature's Constant Gift: A Report on the Water Resource of the Tennessee Valley* (Knoxville: The Authority, 1966)

4. Walter B. Langbein, "Water Yield and Reservoir Storage in the United States," U.S. Geological Survey *Circular* 409, 1959.

5. Arthur Maass, *Muddy Waters: The Army Engineers and the Nation's Rivers* (Cambridge: Harvard University Press, 1951).

   Charles W. McKinley, *Uncle Sam in the Pacific Northwest* (Berkeley: University of California Press, 1952).

   Roscoe C. Martin, Guthrie S. Burkhead, Jesse Burkhead, and Frank J. Munger, *River Basin Administration and the Delaware* (Syracuse: Syracuse University Press, 1960).

   Robert H. Pealy, *Organization for Comprehensive River Basin Planning: The Texas and Southeast Experiences* (Ann Arbor: University of Michigan Governmental Studies, 1964).

6. Walter Firey, *Man, Mind and Land: A Theory of Resource Use* (Glencoe: Free Press, 1960).

   Herbert A. Simon, *Administrative Behavior* (Second edition, New York: Wiley, 1957).

   Philip Selznick, *TVA and the Grass Roots: A Study in the Sociology of Formal Organization* (Berkeley and Los Angeles: University of California Press, 1953).

CHAPTER II

1. Broad descriptions of availability and quality of ground water are given in McGuiness, *The Role of Ground Water in the National Water*

Situation, but there has been no national assessment of the relation of water availability to rural land use.

2. J. J. Moorman, *The Mineral Waters of the United States and Canada* (Baltimore: Kelly & Piet, 1867).

3. J. W. Powell, *Report on the Lands of the Arid Region* (Washington: Government Printing Office, 1879).

4. Since 1957 Colorado has struggled with the definition of guidelines for workable enforcement of ground water law.

5. Evon Z. Vogt and Ray Hyman, *Water Witching, U.S.A.* (Chicago: University of Chicago Press, 1959), pp. 151–79.

6. Changes in the approach to water planning by private consultants are outlined in V. A. Koelzer, "Trends in Planning of Water Resources Projects," *Proceedings of the First Annual Meeting of the American Water Resources Association* (Urbana: The Association, 1965), pp. 135–45.

7. U.S., President's Water Resources Policy Commission, *op. cit.,* pp. 227–37.

8. The most comprehensive appraisal of drainage experience is that by Robert W. Harrison, *Alluvial Empire: A Study of State and Local Efforts Toward Land Development* (Little Rock: Pioneer Press for the Delta Fund, 1961).

9. Harold Hoffman, *Irrigation Development and Public Water Development* (New York: Ronald, 1953).

10. Gilbert F. White, "Industrial Water Supply: A Review," *Geographical Review,* L (1960), pp. 412–30.

Blair T. Bower, "The Economics of Industrial Water Utilization," in Kneese and Smith (eds.), *Water Research* (Baltimore: Johns Hopkins Press, 1966), pp. 143–73.

11. The more comprehensive studies have been by the Corps of Engineers on the impact of the St. Lawrence Seaway on Great Lakes ports traffic.

12. U.S., Tennessee Valley Authority, *Navigation and Economic Growth: Tennessee River Experience* (Knoxville: The Authority, 1966).

13. Carter Goodrich *et al., Canals and American Economic Development* (New York: Columbia University Press, 1961), pp. 246–55.

14. Charles D. Curran, "Evaluation of Federal Navigation Projects," in U.S. Commission on Organization of the Executive Branch of the Government, *Task Force Report on Water Resources and Power* (Washington: Government Printing Office, 1955), pp. 1321–93.

Charles L. Dearing and Wilfred Owen, *National Transportation Policy* (Washington: Brookings Institution, 1949).

U.S., Federal Coordinator of Transportation, *Public Aids to Transportation, III. Water* (Washington: Government Printing Office, 1939).

Marshall E. Dimock, *Developing America's Waterways* (Chicago: University of Chicago Press, 1935).

H. G. Moulton, *The American Transportation Problem* (Washington: Brookings Institution, 1933).

Security Owner's Association, Inc., *A Study of Transportation by Waterways as Related to Competition with Rail Carriers in Continental United States* (New York: The Association, 1932).

Bureau of Railway Economics, *An Economic Survey of Inland Waterway Transportation in the United States* (Washington, 1930).

15. Fogel raises a similar and fundamental question with respect to the effect of railroad building and economic development. While he finds that cheap inland transportation is "a necessary condition for economic growth" he suggests that the condition can be met by any one of several innovations, and that the provision of railways rather than waterways did not affect growth greatly but did influence the paths along which growth took place. Robert William Fogel, *Railroads and American Economic Growth: Essays in Econometric History* (Baltimore: Johns Hopkins Press, 1964), p. 237.

16. Robert S. Kerr, *Land, Wood and Water* (New York: Fleet, 1960), pp. 157–58, 351–53.

17. See U.S., Bureau of Reclamation, *50 Years of Reclamation: Financial Report to the Nation's Stockholders, 1902–1952* (Washington: Government Printing Office, 1952).

Vernon W. Ruttan, *The Economic Demand for Irrigated Acreage: New Methodology and Some Preliminary Projections* (Baltimore: Johns Hopkins Press, 1965).

18. Abel Wolman, "75 Years of Improvement in Water Supply Quality," *Journal of American Water Works Association,* 48 (1956), pp. 905–14.

CHAPTER III

1. Eugene W. Weber and Maynard M. Hufschmidt, "River Basin Planning in the United States," *United States Papers Prepared for the U.N. Conference on the Application of Science and Technology for the Benefit of the Less Developed Areas* (Washington: Government Printing Office, 1963), Vol. I, pp. 299–312.

2. U.S., 71st Congress, 2d Session, House of Representatives, *Report on Tennessee River Basin,* House Document No. 328 (1930).

3. Charles McKinley, "The Valley Authority and Its Alternatives," *American Political Science Review,* 44 (1950), also pp. 567–617 in McKinley, *Uncle Sam in the Pacific Northwest.*

4. United Nations, *Integrated River Basin Development: Report by a Panel of Experts* (New York: United Nations, 1958).

5. Irving K. Fox and Lyle E. Craine, "Organizational Arrangements for Water Development," *Natural Resources Journal* 2 (1962), pp. 1–44.

6. U.S., National Resources Committee, *Regional Planning Part VI—The Rio Grande Joint Investigation in the Upper Rio Grande Basin in Colorado, New Mexico, and Texas 1936–1937* (Washington: Government Printing Office, 1938).

7. Delaware River Basin Commission, *Comprehensive Plan—Phase I* (Philadelphia: The Commission, 1962).

Roscoe C. Martin, et al., *River Basin Administration and the Delaware* (Syracuse: Syracuse University Press, 1960).

8. Much of the experience in the Southeast Basins and in the Texas basins is reviewed in C. E. Kindsvater, editor, *Organization and Methodology for River Basin Planning* (Atlanta: Georgia Institute of Technology, Water Resources Center, 1964).

9. Typical arguments for and against the integration of upstream and downstream measures are found in U.S., *Headwaters Control and Use: A Summary of Fundamental Principles and Their Application in the Conservation and Utilization of Waters and Soils Throughout Headwater Areas* (Washington: Government Printing Office, 1937).

10. Connecticut Commissioner of Agriculture, Conservation and Natural Resources, *Work Plan for Watershed Protection and Flood Prevention, South Branch, Park River Watershed* (1961).

11. U.S., 77th Congress, 2d Session, *Survey Report on Trinity River Watershed*, House Document No. 708 (1942).

12. Luna Leopold and Thomas Maddock Jr., *The Flood Control Controversy: Big Dams, Little Dams, and Land Management* (New York: Ronald Press, 1954).

13. Arthur Maass, *Muddy Waters: The Army Engineers and the Nation's Rivers* (Cambridge: Harvard University Press, 1951).

14. The exchanges between the Departments of Agriculture and Interior over the wisdom of investment in new irrigation enterprises have been numerous over many years. When the Upper Colorado Basin projects were under Congressional discussion the argument led to specification in the Act that new projects feasibility findings should allow a maximum of ten years development, should not count upon surplus crop payments as income, and should be accompanied by Department of Agriculture reports on agricultural aspects. After the reports began appearing with judgments that repayment capacity was very low, the investigations ground to a halt. Even when Agriculture has admitted in its projections of food requirements that additional crop production may in future be required it has not readily assented to the interpretation of arid land representatives that new irrigation would have to help fill the gap.

15. U.S., National Resources Committee, *Deficiencies in Basic Hydrologic Data* (Washington: Government Printing Office, 1936). A comparison report by the National Resources Planning Board on *Deficiencies in Hydrologic Research* followed in 1940.

16. Richard Hazen, in *Proceedings of the National Conference on Water Pollution,* p. 460.

17. U.S., Subcommittee on Evaluation Standards, *Proposed Practices for Eco-*

nomic Analysis of River Basin Projects (Washington: Government Printing Office, 1958).

18. Arthur Maass, et al., *Design of Water-Resource Systems* (Cambridge: Harvard University Press, 1962).

19. U.S., President's Water Resources Policy Commission, *op. cit.,* pp. 11–12. The Commission emphasized the importance of an independent Board of Review.

20. Hubert Marshall, "Politics and Efficiency in Water Development," in Kneese and Smith, eds., *Water Research,* pp. 291–310.

21. Arthur Maass, "Benefit-cost Analysis: Its Relevance to Public Investment Decisions," *Quarterly Journal of Economics,* 80 (1966), pp. 208–26.

22. Special Sub-Committee of the Water Resources Committee, *Drainage Policy and Projects* (Washington: National Resources Committee, 1936).

23. U.S., 89th Congress, 1st Session, *Hearing on H.R. 4671 and similar bills,* House Committee on Interior and Insular Affairs (August-September 1965).

Owen Stratton and Phillip Sirotkin, *The Echo Park Controversy,* Inter-University Case Program (Alabama: University of Alabama Press).

24. Rachel Carson, *Silent Spring* (New York: Houghton Mifflin, 1962).

25. John V. Krutilla, *The Columbia River Treaty: The Economics of an International River Basin Development* (Baltimore: Johns Hopkins Press, 1967).

26. Marion B. Clawson and Jack L. Knetsch, *Economics of Outdoor Recreation* (Baltimore: Johns Hopkins Press, 1966), pp. 188–90.

27. Lyle E. Craine, "The Muskingum Watershed Controversy District: A Study of Local Control," *Law and Contemporary Problems,* 22 (1957) pp. 378–404.

28. U.S., Tennessee Valley Authority, *Annual Reports* of Fish and Game Branch.

29. NAS-NRC Committee on Water, *Alternatives in Water Management,* pp. 18–19. The same idea finds expression in U.S., 89th Congress, 2d Session, *Civil Works Program of the Corps of Engineers,* Senate Committee on Public Works (1966), p. 19.

30. Executive Order No. 11296, August, 1966. U.S. 89th Congress, 2d Session, House of Representatives, *Report of the Task Force on Federal Flood Control Policy,* House Document 465 (1966).

31. Gilbert F. White, et al., *Changes in Urban Occupance of Flood Plains in the United States,* Research Paper No. 57 (Chicago: University of Chicago Department of Geography, 1957).

Gilbert F. White, "Optimal Flood Damage Management: Retrospect and Prospect," *Water Research,* pp. 251–67.

32. U.S., Inland Waterways Commission, *op. cit.*

33. E. F. McCarthy, in "Flood Control with Special Reference to the Missis-

sippi River," *Transactions American Society of Civil Engineers,* 93, Paper 1709, pp. 655–969.

34. When a young officer of the National Resources Planning Board suggested at a planning conference in 1937 that further federal investment in engineering measures in Los Angeles should be contingent upon enactment by responsible local and state agencies of measures to prevent further encroachment on flood plains to be protected with federal largess, the public reaction was hostile.

35. Editorial in *Engineering News-Record* (1937).

36. Gilbert F. White, *Human Adjustment to Floods,* Research Paper No. 29 (Chicago: University of Chicago Department of Geography, 1942).

37. W. G. Hoyt and Walter B. Langbein, *Floods* (Princeton: Princeton University Press, 1955).

38. A. J. Gray, "Planning for Local Flood Damage Prevention," *American Institute of Planners Journal,* 22 (1956), pp. 11–16.

39. U.S., 86th Congress, 1st Session, A Program for Reducing the National Flood Damage Potential, *Senate Committee on Public Works Print,* 1959.

40. Gilbert F. White, "Action Program for the States: A New Attack on Flood Losses," *State Government,* 32 (1959), pp. 121–27.

41. U.S., House Document 465, *op. cit.,* pp. 9–10.

42. The Executive Order did not designate the specific agency assignments. These were made by the Bureau of the Budget. In the Task Force report it had been suggested that the Water Resources Council should be expected to exercise new leadership, but it became difficult to define where the Budget's authority stopped and the Council's began. The recommendations calling for Congressional legislation were the only ones on which action had not been taken.

43. Examples of new research on methods of comparison are found in: Leonard Douglas James, *A Time-Dependent Planning Process for Combining Structural Measures, Land Use, and Flood Proofing to Minimize the Economic Cost of Floods* (Stanford: Stanford University Project on Engineering—Economic Planning, 1964).

    John V. Krutilla, "An Economic Approach to Coping with Flood Damage," *Water Resources Research,* 2 (1966), pp. 183–90.

    Robert C. Lind, *The Nature of Flood Control Benefits and the Economics of Flood Protection* (Stanford: Stanford University Institute for Mathematical Studies in the Social Sciences, 1966).

CHAPTER IV

1. Irving K. Fox, "Policy Problems in the Field of Water Resources," in Kneese and Smith, eds., *Water Research,* pp. 271–89.

2. U.S. Department of the Interior, Federal Water Pollution Control Admin-

istration, *Guidelines for Establishing Water Quality Standards for Interstate Waters* (Washington, 1966).

3. Henry J. Friendly, "The Federal Administrative Agencies: The Need for Better Definition of Standards," *Harvard Law Review,* 75 (1962), Nos. 5, 6, and 7.

4. Abel Wolman, "Bacterial Standards for Natural Waters," *Sewage and Industrial Wastes,* 22 (1950), 348–49. See also Wolman's "Concept of Policy in the Formulation of So-called Standards of Health and Safety," *Journal of American Water Works Association,* 52 (1960), 1343–48.

5. Senate Select Committee, *Report,* p. 30. See also *Committee Print* No. 32, "A Preliminary Report on the Supply and Demand for Water in the United States as Estimated for 1980 and 2000." The criteria are developed in *Committee Print* No. 29, "Water Requirements for Pollution Abatement."

6. Robert K. Davis, "Planning a Water Quality Management System: The Case of the Potomac Estuary," in Kneese and Smith, eds., *Water Research,* pp. 119–20.

7. All of these are included, for example, in the monitoring system established by the Ohio River Valley Water Sanitation Commission. See annual reports by the Commission.

8. J. E. McKee and H. W. Wolf, eds., *Water Quality Criteria* (Sacramento: California State Water Quality Control Board, 1963).

9. *Public Health Reports,* 29 (1914), 40 (1925), 58 (1943) and 61 (1946), and *Public Health Service Publication* No. 956 (1962).

10. U.S., 76th Congress, 1st Session, National Resources Committee, Water Pollution in the United States: *Third Report of the Special Advisory Committee on Water Pollution,* House Document No. 115 (1939).

11. U.S. Department of Health, Education and Welfare, *Proceedings of the National Conference on Water Pollution* (Washington: Government Printing Office, 1961).

12. Allan V. Kneese, *The Economics of Regional Water Quality Management* (Baltimore: Johns Hopkins Press, 1964).

13. NAS-NRC Committee on Pollution, *Waste Management and Control* (Washington, National Academy of Science—National Research Council, 1966).

14. U.S., Presidents' Science Advisory Committee, Environmental Pollution Panel, *Restoring the Quality of our Environment* (Washington: Government Printing Office, 1965).

15. *Proceedings of National Conference, op. cit.* pp. 500, 508, 532.

16. U.S., National Resources Committee, *Drainage Basin Problems and Programs* (Washington: Government Printing Office, 1937). A revision was transmitted to the Congress by the President on March 10, 1938.

17. The study by Prof. Albert Lepawsky was begun several years ago and is

not yet complete. It may well throw different interpretations on the history presented here.

18. U.S., Commission on Organization of the Executive Branch of the Government, *Report on Reorganization of the Department of the Interior,* and *Organization and Policy in the Field of Natural Resources* (Washington: Government Printing Office, 1949).

19. Henry M. Jackson, "Water and the Nation," address to American Water Works Association, May 23, 1966.

20. Norman Wengert, *Natural Resources and the Political Struggle* (Garden City: Doubleday, 1955).

21. Under P.L. 1018, 84th Congress, 1956, reservoirs with a storage exceeding 4,000 acre-feet are referred to the Public Work Committees, and lesser projects are referred to the Agriculture Committee of the Congress before being undertaken.

22. U.S., 89th Congress, 2d Session, Insurance and Other Programs for Financial Assistance to Flood Victims, Senate Committee on Banking and Currency, *Committee Print*, 1966.

23. John M. Clark, Eugene L. Grant, and Maurice M. Kelso, *Report of Panel of Consultants on Secondary or Indirect Benefits of Water-Use Projects,* mimeo (Washington: Bureau of Reclamation, June 26, 1952).

24. Maynard Hufschmidt, John Krutilla, and Julius Margolis, *Report of Panel of Consultants on Standards and Criteria for Formulating and Evaluating Federal Water Resources Developments,* mimeo (Washington: Bureau of the Budget, 1961).

25. Robert H. Pealy, *Organization for Comprehensive River Basin Planning: The Texas and Southeast Experiences* (Ann Arbor: Institute of Public Administration, 1964).

26. *Proceedings of the National Symposium on Quality Standards for Natural Waters* (Ann Arbor: The University of Michigan School of Public Health, 1966).

27. Kneese, *op. cit.,* and *Water Pollution: Economic Aspects and Research Needs* (Washington: Resources for the Future, 1962).

28. Robert K. Davis, "Cleaning up the Potomac Estuary: How Wide a Range of Choice?" *Annual Report* (Washington: Resources for the Future, 1965).

29. U.S., Federal Security Agency, Public Health Service, *Water Pollution in the United States: A report on the polluted condition of our waters and what is needed to restore their quality* (Washington: Government Printing Office, 1951).

30. "Ten Years of Progress in Pollution Abatement," *Public Works* (1965), July.

31. Gilbert F. White, "Formation and Role of Public Attitudes," in Jarrett, ed. *Environmental Quality in a Growing Economy* (Baltimore: Johns Hopkins Press, 1966), pp. 105–27.

32. See the papers by Allen V. Kneese, Ralph Turvey, and M. Mason Gaffney in Jarrett, ed., *Environmental Quality in a Growing Economy*, pp. 47–60, 69–101.

33. U.S., Outdoor Recreation Resources Review Commission, *Outdoor Recreation for America* (Washington: Government Printing Office, 1962). See also Study Reports 5 and 21.

34. For a spectrum of reactions to the Corps plans see U.S. Board of Engineers for Rivers and Harbors, U.S. Army, *Public Hearing on the Potomac River Basin Report,* mimeo, 3 volumes (September, 1963).

35. Davis, *op. cit.*

CHAPTER V

1. Ashley L. Schiff, *Fire and Water: Scientific Heresy in the Forest Service* (Cambridge: Harvard University Press, 1962).

2. U.S. Geological Survey, Preliminary Statement on White Mountains, mimeo, *Forest Service Report,* 13 (1911).

3. W. G. Hoyt and H. C. Troxell, *Transactions of the American Society of Civil Engineers,* 149 (1939), pp. 1–111.

4. For a discussion of types of watershed experiments see L. T. Kelly and L. M Glymph Jr., "Experimental Watersheds and Hydrologic Research," Gentbrugg: International Association for Scientific Hydrology, *Publication 66* (1966) I, pp. 5–11. A further review of experiments in watershed studies is in the papers of the *Proceedings of the International Symposium on Forest Hydrology* (New York: Pergamon Press, 1967).

5. Herbert C. Storey, Robert L. Hobba, and J. Marvin Rosa, "Hydrology of Forest Lands and Rangelands," Chow, ed., *Handbook of Applied Hydrology* (New York: McGraw Hill, 1964). See also the bibliographies published by the Forest Service on *Forest and Range Influences Publications* for 1905–63, 1964, and 1965.

6. Tennessee Valley Authority, *Reforestation and Erosion Control Influences upon the Hydrology of the Pine Tree Branch Watershed,* 1941–60 (Kingsville, TVA, 1962).

7. A special sub-committee of the Water Resources Committee prepared working papers which were not published but which summed up the view that upstream works would not be sufficiently reliable to warrant modifying the design of downstream works.

8. The papers by Dubrevil (54–63), Laszlotty (185–89), and Zeleny (474–79) in IASH *Publication 66* illustrate problems raised by national programs going back to the turn of the century.

9. Much of the early European study turned on effects of vegetation upon sediment movement and torrents. For example M. P. Mougin, *La Restauration des Alpes* (Paris: Imprimerie Nationale, 1931).

10. Soil Conservation Service, *National Engineering Handbook*, Section 4, Hydrology, revised from time to time.

11. See C. H. Wadleigh, et al., "Soil characteristics in the hydrologic continum," and "Soil science in relation to water resources development: I. Watershed protection and flood abatement," *Soil Science Society of America Proceedings*, 30 (1966), pp. 418–24.

12. National Science Foundation, annual reports on *Weather Modification*, 1958 to date.

13. U.S., Special Commission on Weather Modification, *Weather and Climate Modification* (Washington: National Science Foundation, 1965).

U.S., Advisory Committee on Weather Control, *Final Report* (Washington: Government Printing Office, 1957), 2 volumes.

Panel on Weather and Climate Modification, *Weather and Climate Modification: Problems and Prospects* (Washington: National Academy of Sciences—National Research Council, 1966), 2 volumes.

W. R. D Sewell, ed., *Human Dimensions of Weather Modification*, University of Chicago Department of Geography Research Papers, No. 105 (Chicago: 1966).

14. D. L. Gilman, James R. Hibbs, and Paul L. Laskin, *Weather and Climate Modification* (Washington: Weather Bureau, 1965).

15. "Biological Aspects of Weather Modification," *Bulletin of the Ecological Society of America* (March, 1966).

16. Sheppard T. Powell, "Demineralization of Saline Waters," White, ed., *The Future of Arid Lands* (Washington: A.A.A.S., 1957), pp. 257–71.

17. Louis Koenig, "The Economics of Water Sources," *The Future of Arid Lands, op. cit.,* pp. 321–28.

18. All quotations are from the *New York Times* for the days indicated.

19. U.S., Office of Saline Water, *Saline Water Conversion Program Research and Development Project Reports* (Washington: Department of the Interior).

20. U.S., Federal Council for Science and Technology, *A Ten-Year Program of Federal Water Resources Research* (Washington: Government Printing Office, 1966), pp. 31–32.

21. F. M. Middleton, "Operating Experiences of Advanced Waste Treatment Plants," *National Symposium on Quality Standards*, pp. 169–76.

Walter J. Weber, Jr., and Peter F. Atkins, Jr., "Physical Separation Methods for Advanced Treatment of Wastewaters," *op. cit.* pp. 137–53.

22. U.S., Office of Water Resources Research, *Cooperative Water Resources Research and Training: 1965 Annual Report* (Washington: Department of the Interior, 1965).

CHAPTER VI

1. Since the lecture the Supreme Court has released the report of Albert B. Maris, its Special Master on *Wisconsin, Minnesota, Ohio and Pennsyl-*

vania v. State of Illinois and the Metropolitan Sanitary District of Greater Chicago, December 8, 1966 (Philadelphia: Legal Intelligencer). This is an admirable review of the points at issue in the case.

2. U.S., 90th Congress, 1st Session, *Report of the Committee on Public Works on Revising and Extending the Appalachian Regional Development Act of 1965,* Senate Report 159, 1967, 14–15. The Corps of Engineers is given the difficult task of harmonizing regional development and national river basin planning.

3. Jack Hirshleifer, J. C. De Haven, and J. W. Milliman, *Water Supply, Economics, Technology and Policy* (Chicago: University of Chicago Press, 1960).

4. Public Administration Service, *Governmental Administration of Water Resources in the Chicago Metropolitan Area* (Chicago: P.A.S., 1963).

5. Illinois Division of Waterways, *Report on Plan for Flood Control and Drainage Development, Salt Creek, Cook and Du Page Counties* (Springfield: State of Illinois, 1958). The Cook County Forest Preserve District replied with a report by Consoer, Townsend and Associates, *Flood Control Survey and Report for Salt Creek* (1959).

6. John R. Sheaffer, "The Use of Flood Maps in Northeastern Illinois," *Highway Record No. 58* (Washington: National Academy of Sciences, 1964).

7. Testimony of William C. Ackermann, Chief, State Water Survey, in hearings on *Illinois v. Michigan, et al.,* October term, 1959.

8. John R. Sheaffer and Arthur J. Zeizel, *The Water Resource in Northeastern Illinois: Planning its Use,* Technical Report No. 4 (Chicago: Northeastern Illinois Planning Commission, 1966).

9. Lyle E. Craine notes from his analysis of British experience in water management that it is possible for many water management responsibilities to be carried by government agencies which build the water activities into other management functions. In Britain, stress is placed on how the specialized water agencies, such as the river authorities, collaborate with those other public entities.

10. Edward A. Ackerman and George O. G. Löf, *Technology in American Water Development* (Baltimore: Johns Hopkins Press, 1959).

11. The problems of forecasting technological change and its impacts are discussed in U.S., National Commission on Technology, Automation, and Economic Process, *Technology and American Society* (Washington: Government Printing Office, 1966). See especially Volume V, pp. 259–90.

12. The Delaware Basin has enjoyed a series of efforts to inform and mobilize citizen opinion on basin problems under the Delaware River Basin Advisory Committee, Delaware River Basin Research, Inc., and, more recently, the Water Resources Association of the Delaware River Basin.

13. League of Women Voters Education Fund, *The Big Water Fight* (Brattleboro: Stephen Greene Press, 1966).

Selected References on
American Water Management

The Water Resource

Langbein, Walter B. and William G. Hoyt, *Water Facts for the Nation's Future: Uses and Benefits of Hydrologic Data Programs*, New York: Ronald, 1959.

Leopold, Luna B. and Walter B. Langbein, *A Primer on Water*, Washington: U.S. Geological Survey, 1960.

Linsley, Ray K., Max A. Kohler and Joseph L. H. Paulhus, *Hydrology for Engineers*, New York: McGraw-Hill, 1958.

McGuinness, C. L., *The Role of Ground Water in the National Water Situation*, U.S. Geological Survey Water Supply Paper 1800, Washington, 1963.

Miller, David, et al., *Water Atlas of the United States*, Port Washington: Water Information Center, Inc., 1963.

Piper, A. M., *Has the United States Enough Water?*, U.S. Geological Survey Water Supply Paper 1797, Washington, 1965.

Thomas, Harold E., *The Conservation of Ground Water*, New York: McGraw-Hill, 1951.

Wolman, Abel, "Water," in National Academy of Sciences—National Research Council, *Natural Resources*, Washington: NAS-NRC, 1962.

Technology

Ackerman, Edward, and George Löf, *Technology in American Water Development*, Baltimore: Johns Hopkins Press, 1959.

Chow, Ven Te, ed., *Handbook of Applied Hydrology*, New York: McGraw-Hill, 1964.

Basic Federal Reports

Commission on the Organization of the Executive Branch, *Organization and Policy in the Field of Natural Resources*, Washington: Government Printing Office, 1949.

Commission on the Organization of the Executive Branch, *Task Force Report on Water Resources and Power*, 3 volumes, Washington: Government Printing Office, 1955.

Department of Health, Education, and Welfare, *Proceedings of the National Conference on Water Pollution,* Washington: Government Printing Office, 1961.

Inland Waterways Commission, *Preliminary Report,* Washington: Government Printing Office, 1908.

National Conservation Commission, *Report,* U.S. Senate Doc. 676, 60th Congress, 2d session, Feb. 1909.

National Resources Board, *Report,* Part III: "Report of the Water Planning Committee," Washington: Government Printing Office, 1934.

National Resources Committee, *Drainage Basin Problems and Programs,* Washington: Government Printing Office, 1935. Rev. ed., 1936.

National Waterways Commission, *Final Report,* Washington: Government Printing Office, 1912.

Powell, J. W., *Report on the Lands of the Arid Region,* Washington: Government Printing Office, 1879.

President's Materials Policy Commission, *Resources for Freedom,* Washington: Government Printing Office, 1952.

President's Water Resources Policy Commission, *A Water Policy for the American People* (Vol. 1), *Ten Rivers in America's Future* (Vol. 2), *Water Resources Law* (Vol. 3), Washington: Government Printing Office, 1950.

Presidential Advisory Committee on Water Resources Policy, *Water Resources Policy,* Washington: Government Printing Office, 1955.

Subcommittee on Evaluation Standards of Inter-Agency Committee on Water Resources, *Proposed Practices for Economic Analysis on River Basin Projects,* Washington: Government Printing Office, 1958.

U.S., 87th Congress, 1st Session, *Report of Senate Select Committee on National Water Resources,* Senate Report No. 29, with 32 Committee Prints, Washington: Government Printing Office, 1961.

U.S., 87th Congress, 2d Session, *Policies, Standards and Procedures in the Formulation, Evaluation and Review of Plans for Use and Development of Water and Related Land Resources,* Senate Document 97, Washington: Government Printing Office, 1962.

U.S., 89th Congress, 2d Session, *Civil Works Program of the Corps of Engineers: A Report to the Secretary of the Army by the Civil Works Study Board,* Senate Committee on Public Works, Washington: Committee Print, 1966.

U.S., 89th Congress, 2d Session, *A Unified National Program for Managing Flood Losses,* House Document 465, Washington: Government Printing Office, 1966.

U.S., Office of Science and Technology, *Research and Development on Natural Resources,* Report prepared by the Committee on Natural Resources, Federal Council for Science and Technology, Washington: Government Printing Office, 1963.

Selected Basin and State Reports

Delaware River Basin Commission, *Water Resources Program,* Trenton: The Commission, 1965.

Interstate Commission on the Delaware River Basin, *The Delaware River Basin,* Philadelphia: The Commission, 1940.

Morgan, Arthur E., *The Miami Conservancy District,* New York: McGraw-Hill, 1951.

State of California, Department of Water Resources, Division of Resources Planning, *The California Water Plan,* Bulletin No. 3, May, 1957.

U.S. Bureau of Reclamation, *Columbia Basin Joint Investigations,* reports on problem studies, Washington: Government Printing Office, 1942–45.

U.S. Department of the Army, Corps of Engineers, *Delaware River Basin Report,* 11 vols. Washington: Government Printing Office, 1962.

U.S. Department of the Army, Corps of Engineers, *Potomac River Basin Report,* 9 vols. Washington: Government Printing Office, 1963.

U.S. Department of the Interior, *The Colorado River: A Comprehensive Report,* Washington: Government Printing Office, 1946.

U.S. Missouri Basin Survey Commission, *Missouri: Land and Water,* Washington: Government Printing Office, 1953.

U.S. Study Commission—Southeast River Basins, *Plan for Development of the Land and Water Resources of the Southeast River Basins,* The Commission, 1963.

U.S. Study Commission—Texas, *Report* Parts I, II, III, The Commission, 1962, Summary and Recommendations: April, 1962.

U.S. Tennessee Valley Authority, *Report to the Congress on the Unified Development of the Tennessee River System,* Knoxville: The Authority, 1936.

Economic

Ciriacy-Wantrup, S. V., *Resource Conservation,* Berkeley: University of California Press, 1952.

Eckstein, Otto, *Water-Resource Development,* Cambridge: Harvard University Press, 1958.

Fox, Irving K. and Orris C. Herfindahl, "Attainment of Efficiency in Satisfying Demands for Water Resources," *American Economic Review* (1964).

Grant, E. L. and W. G. Ireson, *Principles of Engineering Economy,* 4th Edition, New York: Ronald, 1960.

Haveman, Robert H., *Water Resource Investment in the Public Interest,* Nashville, Tennessee: Vanderbilt, 1965.

Hirshleifer, Jack, James C. De Haven, and Jerome W. Milliman, *Water Supply,* Chicago: University of Chicago Press, 1960.

Hufschmidt, Maynard M., John Krutilla, and Julius Margolis, *Report of Panel of Consultants to the Bureau of the Budget on Standards and Criteria for Formulating and Evaluating Federal Water Resources Developments,* Washington: Bureau of the Budget, 1961.

Kneese, Allen V., *The Economics of Regional Water Quality Management,* Baltimore: Johns Hopkins Press, 1965.

Krutilla, John V. and Otto Eckstein, *Multiple Purpose River Development,* Baltimore: Johns Hopkins Press, 1958.

Maass, Arthur, "Benefit-cost Analysis: Its Relevance to Public Investment Decisions," *Quarterly Journal of Economics,* 80 (1966), pp. 208–26.

——, and Maynard M. Hufschmidt, R. Dorfman, Harold A. Thomas, Jr., Stephen A. Marglin, and Gordon M. Fair, *Design of Water-Resource Systems,* Cambridge: Harvard University Press, 1962.

McKean, Roland N., *Efficiency in Government through Systems Analysis,* New York: Wiley, 1958.

Renshaw, Edward F., *Toward Responsible Government,* Chicago: University of Chicago, the author, 1958.

Smith, Stephen C. and Emery Castle, eds., *Economics and Public Policy in Water Resource Development,* Ames: Iowa State, 1964.

Steiner, P. O., "Choosing Among Alternating Public Investments in the Water Resource Field," *American Economic Review,* 49 (1959), pp. 893–916.

Tolley, G. S. and F. E. Riggs, eds., *Symposium on the Economics of Watershed Planning,* Ames: Iowa State University Press, 1961.

Wollman, Nathaniel, *The Value of Water in Alternative Uses,* Albuquerque: University of New Mexico Press, 1962.

Administrative and Political

Council of State Governments, *State Administration of Water Resources,* Chicago: The Council, 1957.

Craine, Lyle E., "The Muskingum Watershed Conservancy District: A Study of Local Control," *Law and Contemporary Problems,* 22 (Summer, 1957).

Engelbert, Ernest A., "Political Parties and National Resources Policies: An Historical Evaluation, 1790–1950," *Natural Resources Journal,* I (Nov. 1961), pp. 224–56.

Fesler, James W., "National Water Resources Administration," *Law and Contemporary Problems,* 20 (Summer, 1957), pp. 444–71.

Fox, Irving K., "New Horizons in Water Resources Administration," *Public Administration Review,* 25 (1965), pp. 61–69.

——, and Lyle E. Craine, "Organizational Arrangements for Water Development," *Natural Resources Journal,* 2 (1962), pp. 1–44.

——, and Isobel Pickin, *The Upstream-Downstream Flood Control Controversy in the Arkansas-White-Red Basins Survey,* Alabama: University of Alabama Press, 1960.

Hardin, Charles M., *The Politics of Agriculture: Soil Conservation and the Struggle for Power in Rural America,* Glencoe: Free Press, 1952.

Hart, Henry C., "Crisis, Community and Consent in Water Politics," *Law and Contemporary Problems,* 22 (Summer, 1957), pp. 510–37.

———, *The Dark Missouri,* Madison: University of Wisconsin Press, 1957.

Kindsvater, C. E., ed., *Organization and Methodology for River Basin Planning,* Atlanta: Water Resources Center, Georgia Institute of Technology, 1964.

Lepawsky, Albert, "Water Resources and American Federalism," *American Political Science Review,* 44 (1950), pp. 631–49.

Leuchtenburg, William E., "Roosevelt, Norris and the Seven Little TVA's," *Journal of Politics,* 14 (1952), pp. 418–24.

Maass, Arthur, *Muddy Waters: The Army Engineers and the Nation's Rivers,* Cambridge: Harvard University Press, 1951.

———, "Protecting Nature's Reservoir," *Public Policy,* 5 (1954), pp. 71–106.

McKinley, Charles W., "The Valley Authority and its Alternatives," *American Political Science Review,* 44 (1950), pp. 607–31.

———, *Uncle Sam in the Pacific Northwest,* Berkeley: University of California Press, 1952.

Ostrom, Vincent, "State Administration of Natural Resources in the West" (bibl.), *American Political Science Review,* 47 (June, 1953), pp. 478–93.

———, *Water and Politics: A Study of Water Policies and Administration in the Development of Los Angeles,* Los Angeles: Haynes Foundation, 1953.

Pealy, Robert H., *Comprehensive River Basin Planning: The Arkansas-White-Red Basins Inter-Agency Committee Experience,* Ann Arbor: University of Michigan Governmental Studies, 1959.

Schiff, Ashley L., *Fire and Water: Scientific Heresy in the Forest Service,* Cambridge: Harvard University Press, 1962.

Wengert, Norman, *Natural Resources and the Political Struggle,* Garden City: Doubleday, 1955.

Willoughby, William, *The St. Lawrence Waterway: A Study in Politics and Diplomacy,* Madison: University of Wisconsin Press, 1961.

The Tennessee Valley Authority

Clapp, Gordon R., *The TVA, An Approach to the Development of a Region,* Chicago: University of Chicago Press, 1955.

Lilienthal, David E., *TVA, Democracy on the March,* New York: Harper, 1953.

Pritchett, C. Herman, *The Tennessee Valley Authority: A Study in Public Administration,* Chapel Hill: University of North Carolina Press, 1943.

Selznick, Philip, *TVA and the Grass Roots: A Study in the Sociology of Formal Organization,* Berkeley and Los Angeles: University of California Press, 1953.

Water Law

Haber, David, and Stephen W. Bergen, eds., *The Law of Water Allocation in the Eastern United States, Proceedings of a symposium held October, 1956,* New York: Ronald, 1958.

Hutchins, W. A. and H. A. Steele, "Basic Water Rights Doctrines and Their Implications for River Basin Development," *Law and Contemporary Problems,* 22 (1957), pp. 276–300.

Milliman, J. W., "Water Law and Private Decision-Making," *Journal of Law and Economics,* 2 (1959), pp. 41–63.

National Reclamation Association, *Preservation of Integrity of State Water Laws: Report and Recommendations, October, 1943,* n.p. 1943.

Ostrom, Vincent, "1964: Western Water Institutions in a Contemporary Perspective," *Proceedings: Western Interstate Water Conference,* 1964, pp. 22–29, Los Angeles: University of California Water Resources Center, 1964.

Trelease, Frank J., "A Model State Water Code for River Basin Development," *Law and Contemporary Problems,* 22 (1957), pp. 301–22.

———, "Policies for Water Law: Property Rights, Economic Forces and Public Regulations," *Natural Resources Journal,* 5 (1965), pp. 1–48.

Wiel, Samuel C., *Water Rights in the Western States,* San Francisco: Bancroft Whitney, 3rd ed., 1911.

U.S. Department of Agriculture, Economic Research Service, Farm Economics Division, Miscellaneous Publication No. 921, *State Water Rights Laws and Related Subjects: A Bibliography,* Washington: Government Printing Office, 1962.

General

Ackerman, Edward A., "Questions for Designers of Future Water Policy," *Journal of Farm Economics,* 38 (1956), pp. 971–80.

Hays, Samuel, *Conservation and the Gospel of Efficiency,* Cambridge: Harvard University Press, 1959.

Jarrett, Henry, ed., *Perspectives on Conservation: Essays on America's Natural Resources,* Baltimore: Johns Hopkins Press, 1958.

———, *Comparisons in Resource Management,* Baltimore: Johns Hopkins Press, 1961.

King, Judson, *The Conservation Fight from Theodore Roosevelt to the Tennessee Valley Authority,* Washington: Public Affairs Press, 1959.

Leuchtenburg, William E., *Flood Control Politics, The Connecticut River Valley Problem, 1927–1950,* Cambridge: Harvard University Press, 1953.

Moreell, Ben, *Our Nation's Water Resources—Policies and Politics,* Chicago: University of Chicago Law School, 1956.

National Academy of Sciences—National Research Council, *Alternatives in Water Management,* Washington: NAS-NRC, 1966.

Newell, Frederick Haynes, *Water Resources, Present and Future Uses,* New Haven: Yale University Press, 1913.

Swain, Donald C., *Federal Conservation Policy, 1921–33,* Berkeley: University of California Press, 1963.

U.S. Department of Agriculture, *Yearbook of Agriculture, 1953: Water,* Washington: Government Printing Office.

Van Hise, Charles R., *The Conservation of Natural Resources in the United States,* New York: Macmillan, 1915.

Selected Events in American Water Management

1808   Gallatin's report on roads and canals.

1817   Construction of Erie Canal authorized by New York State.

1850   Federal government assumes responsibility for navigation improvements.

1873   Timber Culture Act authorizes tree planting to affect climate.

1874   Report of Windom Committee to the Senate.

1879   Powell's report on policy for use of arid lands.

1879   Mississippi River Commission established to coordinate lower Mississippi flood control.

1894   Cary Act provides for cooperation with states in irrigation district development.

1901   National Rivers and Harbors Congress established.

1902   Reclamation Act establishes federal support for irrigation planning and construction.

1908   Conference of Governors on Conservation.

1908   Preliminary report of the Inland Waterways Commission.

1909   Report of the National Conservation Commission.

1911   Weeks Act authorizes national forest purchases to assist in runoff regulation and for other purposes.

1914   Ohio Conservancy Act authorizes districts for basin-wide flood control.

1917   Federal government assumes responsibility for Lower Mississippi flood control.

1920   Federal Power Act licenses power sites for the coordinated development of water resources for power and related purposes.

1927   Corps of Engineers authorized to prepare "308" reports on navigation, irrigation, flood control, and power development of designated basins.

1928   Boulder Canyon Project Act adopts the multiple-purpose idea for Hoover Dam.

1928   Lower Mississippi Flood Control Act provides for unified levee and floodway program.

1933   Public Works Administration begins major program of construction of water projects.

1933   Tennessee Valley Authority established as a government corporation.

1934   National Resources Board created. Subsequently, National Resources Committee and National Resources Planning Board.

1934   Lower Colorado River Authority established as a state agency on an intrastate stream.

1935   Soil Conservation Service established in Department of Agriculture.

1936   Flood Control Act assigns primary responsibility for flood protection on the main streams to Corps of Engineers, and in upper watersheds to Department of Agriculture.

1936   Interstate Commission on the Delaware River Basin (Incodel) established.

1937   Pittman-Robertson Act allocates federal excise tax for wildlife restoration through state projects.

1938   Cost of reservoirs for flood control made wholly federal.

1939   Reclamation Project Act strengthens Bureau of Reclamation planning functions.

1943   National Resources Planning Board killed by Congress.

1943   Federal Inter-Agency River Basin Committee (FIARBC) created.

1944   Flood Control Act approves Pick-Sloan plan for development of Missouri Basin, and requires coordination of basin reports by interested agencies.

1945   Missouri Basin Regional Inter-Agency Basin Committee established.

1946   Columbia River Regional Inter-Agency Basin Committee established.

1948   Pacific Southwest Regional Inter-Agency Basin Committee established.

1948   Water Pollution Act establishes study program and grants for waste treatment.

1949   First Hoover Commission Report recommends reorganization of natural resources functions in Department of Interior, and transfer of civil responsibilities of Corps of Engineers to it.

1950   Arkansas—White-Red Regional Inter-Agency Basin Committee established.

1950   New England—New York Regional Inter-Agency Basin Committee established.

1950   Dingell-Johnson Act authorizes federal aid for restoration of fresh water fish.

1950   President's Water Resources Policy Commission reports on policy needs.

1950   Proposed practices for economic analysis of river basin projects—Report of a subcommittee of the Federal Inter-Agency Committee (the "Green Book").

1954   Watershed Protection and Flood Prevention Act (P.L. 566) establishes technical and financial aid to local organizations for watershed work plans.

1955   Report of the Presidential Advisory Committee on Water Resources Policy.

1955   Second Hoover Commission reports.

1957 State of California publishes State Water Plan.

1958 Amendment to Fish and Wildlife Conservation Act authorizes studies of effects of water projects on fish and wildlife.

1960 National Conference on Water Pollution reviews need for new policy.

1961 Senate Select Committee on National Water Resources reports on assessment of water needs and of ways of meeting them.

1961 Farmers Home Administration authorized to make loans and grants for rural water supply.

1962 Texas Drainage Basins U.S. Study Commission reports.

1962 Delaware River Basin Commission created by four states and federal government.

1962 Senate Document No. 97 specifies policies and procedures for formulation and evaluation of water plans.

1963 Southeast River Basins U.S. Study Commission reports.

1964 Wilderness Act authorizes reserve of wilderness areas.

1964 Water Resources Research Act authorizes support for state water centers and for non-federal research activities.

1965 Water Resources Planning Act establishes Water Resources Council and authorizes creation of regional commissions.

1965 Land and Water Conservation Fund Act authorizes land planning and acquisition for recreational and wildlife use.

1965 Water Quality Act.

1966 Report of National Science Foundation Special Commission on Weather Modification.

Index